POSTCARDS
— FROM THE —
FRONT
1914–1919

Kate J. Cole

AMBERLEY

*This book is dedicated with love to my dad
and also to his dad, Private George Parnall Cole of the York &
Lancaster Regiment, who during the Hundred Days Offensive received
a Blighty wound in France on 14 October 1918, aged just nineteen.*

November 2014's astonishing display 'Blood-swept Land and Seas of Red' depicting the walls of the ancient Tower of London haemorrhaging the nation's blood. The display contained 888,246 individually created poppies, each poppy representing the British and Colonial military dead of the First World War. In among this sea of blood are four poppies representing the dead from the author's family.

First published 2016

Amberley Publishing
The Hill, Stroud
Gloucestershire, GL5 4EP

www.amberleybooks.com

British Library Cataloguing in Publication Data.
A catalogue record for this book is available from the British Library.

ISBN 978 1 4456 3500 2 (print)
ISBN 978 1 4456 3521 7 (ebook)

Typesetting and Origination by Amberley Publishing.
Printed in Great Britain.

Contents

"Somme" Post Office.

Introduction

From the end of the nineteenth century onwards, postmen delivered daily postcards sent by people to their family and friends to houses all across Britain. Postcards were the social media and text messages of their day, short messages sent to loved ones to keep families and friends in touch with each other. Just as today's digital age brings instant satisfaction, postcards performed the same task a hundred years ago. Local postcards often arrived on the very same day that they were posted and no more than the next day for postcards sent further afield within Britain.

Postcards had two tempting appeals: short messages could be written to keep in touch or write brief items of news (no need to write a lengthy time-consuming letter), and a pretty picture to go along with the message. Postcards with pictures illustrating just about every subject and theme were produced all round Britain (and the world), from topographical real photographic postcards of street scenes in towns and villages, to pictures of anthropomorphic animals dressed as humans. It would seem that no subject was left untouched by postcard publishers. Many people avidly collected these postcards and stored their hoard of pretty pictures safely in postcard albums. It is for this reason that many postcards have survived remarkably intact, despite the passage of time. Whereas a letter may have been thrown out many decades ago, postcards, with their appealing pictures on the front, have been kept.

The so-called 'Golden Age' of postcard production was undoubtedly the early twentieth century. However, the sending and receiving of postcards reached a new peak during the First World War. The safe delivery of post sent to and from men (and women) who were serving overseas for King and Country between 1914 and 1919 was essential. Post from home was vital to the morale of the men and women who were serving in a treacherous and dangerous war, far from home.

During the First World War, so much mail was posted to and from troops that by December 1914. a new central sorting office had to be built. The Home Depot was constructed in London's Regent's Park covering 5 acres of land in the world's largest (at that time) wooden structure. At its peak, it handled 12 million letters/postcards and 1 million parcels each week. By the end of the war, the Home Depot's employees consisted mainly of female workers and there were approximately 2,500 employees. After the depot had processed the letters, postcards and parcels, they then had to be dispatched for their final destinations.[1]

Edwin Pratt, writing in his 1921 book *British Railways and the Great War*, stated that from early 1915 until November 1918, a daily train consisting of between thirty to thirty-five large box-trucks pulled into Victoria Station at 11 a.m. Bags of outgoing mail were continuously loaded into this train until 11:30 p.m., when it was then dispatched to Folkestone with its final destination being France. This happened every single day without fail, and sometimes the loads were so large that two trains had to be used. Pratt estimated that the total number of wartime sacks of mail dispatched from just Victoria Station bound for France was 10,463,834, weighing a total of 324,596 tons. The yearly totals for this staggering number of sacks are 25,785 for the five months of war in 1914 (dating from before the instigation of the special daily train). In 1915 there were 177,220 sacks (a low number because the early months of this year did not have the benefit of the daily special train), in 1916 3,023,851 sacks, 4,210,805 in 1917 and 3,026,173 for the first eleven months of 1918. These are figures for only the outgoing post from Britain to the Western Front. Other trains and stations throughout London had similar operations to get Britain's mail to Southampton and ultimately to troops serving in the rest of the world. Similar numbers of incoming post from overseas arrived in Victoria, Charing Cross and Cannon Street train stations, for processing in Regent's Park's Home Depot.[2] Because of German U-boat activity, wherever possible, mail to the rest of the world had to be transported overland via the western front between 1915 and 1917, after which time conveys were put in place to protect ships.

In among this vast amount of mail were all the postcards detailed within this book, approximately 200 messages written onto postcards during the First World War – a tiny insignificant drop in that vast ocean of mail. The end date of this book, 1919, is intentional; the majority of men were not demobbed and sent back to Britain until 1919 (and even on into the 1920s) and so continued to send their postcards home from abroad. I have also purposely kept to British postcards sent to and from the Western Front (France and Belgium) or sent from within Britain. The omission of Britain's Commonwealth countries, her allies, and other areas of conflict (such as the Eastern Front and Africa) is also deliberate. There simply is not enough room in one single book to detail messages from all the combatant nations of the First World War and all its theatres of war.

In many respects, this book is more about what was not written in the messages and reading between the lines of the messages, many of which were often cheerful and putting a 'brave face' on an appalling and unimaginable situation. The conditions of trench warfare, hand-to-hand fighting, the long painful marches, the fear and helplessness were rarely, if ever, mentioned. These postcards were not written in the comfort of a warm safe house but written whenever possible, after days and nights of fighting and marching, in terrible conditions.

In addition, every single postcard sent from overseas to Britain was censored to ensure that if the post fell into enemy hands, nothing could be gleaned from it. Many a postcard was sent home with the heading 'Somewhere in France' or 'From one in Belgium'. The majority of postcards sent were simply a means of keeping a connection between family and friends. People were inclined to write their news in longer, more detailed letters home, which, in the main, have not survived the last hundred years in such large quantities as postcards. Countless postcards have short messages similar to 'Just a card to let you know I am going on quite well at present'. Or 'We are having fine weather here and I hope that you are having the same.' From reading Britain's postcards during the First World War, it would seem that the entire country and all its armed services were obsessed with the weather. However, weather was a crucial obsession and observation when your very life depended on reasonable conditions while fighting in the water-logged trenches in war-torn France, or sailing on a ship across a perilous sea and into a warzone.

Moreover, this is a one-way conversation for the modern-day reader; the postcards sent from Britain to men serving abroad have not survived in the same quantities as postcards sent back to Britain. Many postcards and letters sent to soldiers would have been destroyed at the time, deemed too heavy or bulky to keep and add to an existing load when men were marching from place to place, or running into battle, carrying their worldly possessions on their back.

Most postcards in this book are single cards, with scant personal details leading to no possible chance of being able to identify the sender. Many of these single postcards would have once been eagerly collected during the war and kept as prizes within life-long personal possessions. But with the passage of a hundred years, these collections have now been split and scattered to the four winds, so that all that remains of one person's war are mere fragments. However, I was able to identify the extensive postcard collections of three people – the Voluntary Aid Detachment nurse Clara Woolnough who nursed wounded men during the Battles of the Somme, and the two Pullen brothers, Reginald who fought on land during the Battles of the Somme and the Third Battle of Ypres, and his brother Charles who was involved in aerial combat in the skies above the Western Front. Their stories, which are just three among the countess millions of accounts of individual heroism from all sides, were so remarkable that I have expanded their postcard messages to include research from war diaries, newspaper accounts and other contemporary sources.

Thus, this book is not an account of the war to end wars. Nor is it an explanation of the battles and military history of the First World War. It is not even a history of the millions of postcards produced, printed and posted during that war. Quite simply, this book is the story, in their own words and pictures, of a handful of British men and women who went to war for their King and Country 100 years ago.

> They shall grow not old, as we that are left grow old:
> Age shall not weary them, nor the years condemn.
> At the going down of the sun and in the morning
> We will remember them.
> 'For the Fallen', Robert Laurence Binyon (1869–1943)

Kate Cole
Maldon, Summer 2016
www.essexvoicespast.com

Quick, Give me some news from you.

See how gay we are when the sargent gives us our letters. See how sad we are, when we don't have any mail.
For God sake please write carefully the adress to facilitate the « job » of our P O. Sargent

Chapter 1
Keep the Home Fires Burning

Worcester Regiment in the grounds of Maldon Workhouse (Essex), 1915.

On Tuesday 4 August 1914, Britain declared war on Germany. The day before, the last day of peace, had been a Bank Holiday Monday and a glorious sunny day in Britain. Many British families, although aware of the intensifying crisis in Europe that had started in June with the assassination of Archduke Franz Ferdinand in Sarajevo, had spent their time off work enjoying a leisurely day with their families. The day after the Declaration of War, Field Marshal Kitchener, Earl Kitchener of Khartoum and Broome, became the Secretary of State for War. He immediately issued orders for soldiers who were already regulars or reservists in the British Army to mobilise, and preparations commenced for sending this pre-war army to France. By 23 August 1914, the British Expeditionary Force (the BEF) were in position to fight their first battle with the German Army at Mons. The original BEF was a single army and small in size, consisting of four infantry divisions, two cavalry divisions and various other units such as lines of communication, Corps and HQ. Two other infantry divisions were initially kept back to protect Britain as the War Office initially feared a German attack on British soil, but one of these divisions was later deployed to France and arrived there by 26 August 1914. [1:1]

Immediately upon his appointment as the Secretary of State for War, Kitchener, knowing that this small pre-war army was not large enough for a full-scale land war with Germany, made plans to expand the army. He sent out his famous 'Call to Arms – Briton Wants You Join Your Country's Army!' on 11 August 1914 and within two weeks 100,000 men had volunteered to join Kitchener's Army.[1:2] Thus started the year-by-year increase of the armed services, which further expanded with the introduction of conscription in 1916. By the end of the war, four years later in 1918, nearly a quarter of all men within Britain had served in the country's armed forces.[1:3]

Throughout the war, Britain was full of soldiers from numerous battalions and regiments who were in the process of being trained in Britain and then deployed overseas. The postcards in this chapter are the messages from some of those soldiers.

At the beginning of August 1914, Harry, writing to his sweetheart in Norwich, was stationed in Shenfield in Essex. He did not state his regiment on his postcard, but his messages show that he was first in Harwich, then in Shenfield and by the end of August in Drayton, and he was awaiting news about when he would be leaving for France.

Brentwood, Friday evening, 14 August 1914. Dear G. I must send a card to thank you for letters, it was very good to read them. I will try and write you all the news later. I just returned from seeing the Prince of Wales out walking last night. We have more freedom here than at Harwich. I am alright & feel ever so well. We drill on this common [Shenfield] each morning. Hope you are having nice trips & feel the benefit of your holiday. Goodbye, Harry

Drayton 20 August 1914. Dear G, I arrived back here [Drayton] alright at 9:40 and got in without any questions. We have been on a route march today about 12 miles. Hope you had a nice time at Lowestoft. No more definite news yet. The heather and bracken we saw today was splendid. Goodbye Harry

Harry's reference to the Prince of Wales (later King Edward VIII) related to the Prince who had joined his new regiment, 1st Grenadier Guards, at Warley Barracks in Brentwood on the 10 August 1914. Newspapers reported that the Prince's first day with the regiment was spent marching in Brentwood, and then performing duties at his barracks.[1:4]

By the end of August 1914, thousands upon thousands of men had joined the army; eager to fight for King and country. However, the majority of these new recruits were untrained men, so there was an urgent need for rapid training, especially in the use of rifles. Field Marshal Kitchener authorised the National Rifle Association to form a Corps of Expert Service Rifle Shots consisting of veteran crack-shot instructors with their duty being to rapidly train these new recruits. In late August 1914, newspapers reported that Bisley Camp in Surrey, which was then the headquarters of the National Rifle Association, had been turned into vast military training camp.[1:5]

Bert was one such soldier in training at Bisley at the start of the war. His message is evocative of the enthusiastic and excited 'it'll be over by Christmas' mood prevalent at the start of the war in August 1914, with young men eager to fight abroad, anxious that the war would be over before they could get there.

By the following years, the training camp at Bisley was well established. The bottompostcard shows the Machine Gun Wing who trained there. Hopefully the unknown writer passed his exam on machine guns and tactics.

Postmarked Bisley Camp, Woking, Surrey, 31 August 1914
A. F. Liddel, No. 3 Company, Post Office Rifles, Bisley, Dear B, Going strong and feeling fine. The whole battalion have been asked to volunteer for the Front and have done so. You bet. Will write soon. Love to all Bert

Bisley, Machine Gun Wing 26 May 1916
Busy swotting for written paper on machine gun and tactics for tomorrow. So sorry I've not time for a letter. Will try to meet you on Saturday. Goodbye for now. Ever yours

THE 'GENERAL' ISN'T PLEASED WITH THE RESULT OF THE MILITARY MANŒUVRES!

Left: Postmarked Bournemouth, 20 October 1914

Dear Charlie, hope you are getting better and having a skirmish around. We are having some champion weather here it is enough to roast one during the day but blooming cold first thing of the morning and night. Will you send me some brown paper on to wrap my clothes in also my body belt. Don't send me any postcards on because they will only get destroyed. Nowhere to put them. We are having some very heavy work now we have got us rifles, so we will soon be after the Germans. Remember me to Bill and the Mrs. From your old pal, Reg. Send some string.

Below: Gymnastic Class at Exercise Royal Horse Guards

Postmarked London 30 November 1914: Dear Gertrude, as promised I am just spending a halfpenny on this. I think you had better come and have a week or two in London. It is a fine place. I am now a full trooper. Kind regards Harold

Trooper Harold Draycott, regimental number 2204 of the Royal Regiment of Horse Guards, was based in the Albany Barracks in Regents Park, London. He wrote to his sweetheart in Leeds, sending her a picture of his gymnastic class.

GYMNASTIC CLASS AT EXERCISE. R.H.GDS.

Conditions were tough in the military camps and the weather made these conditions harsher. Arthur sent home a picture of his camp in Hornchurch, Essex under snow. The perfect flock of birds flying high above the camp painted on later by the photographer.

The Camp under Snow.

Above: Hornchurch Camp
  A view of our camp under snow. It looks alright does it not? It was very cold. Arthur

Right: George was at Larkhill on Salisbury Plain at the School of Instruction for Royal Horse and Field Artillery. The School was founded in 1915 and is still operational today as the Royal School of Artillery.[1:6]

School of Instruction, R.F.A and R.H.A, 14 Camp, Lark Hill, Salisbury Plain. Dear M, arrived here tonight. Have found some pals already. It's not a bad place down here. Have just had tea in the Sergeant's mess. Last night I stayed at Thompson's the night. The weather is lovely here. Will send particulars in a day or two. Best love to all. George

Nerves

Left: An unknown soldier was training at the large military camp at Bordon and Longmoor in Hampshire when he sent his wife a patriotic postcard of Field Marshal Earl Kitchener.

10 May 1917: My darling wife, this time we move off in the morning at quarter to five and leave Bordon station at 6am. We got inspected by the Colonel this afternoon. He said we are a fine body of men and he was proud of us. He said we were lucky to be on the broad gauge railway as we are well away from the Front. I don't know whether I told you or not, but there is [sic] small railways near the trenches. They lose a terrible amount of men every week. I think you was right when you often said that if I went, I would be lucky enough to come back & I think we are lucky to get on.

Below: His Majesty the King Inspects Troops on Salisbury Plain
Postmarked Larkhill Camp, 29 July 1915: Dear friend. We have got our last leave. I shall be coming Friday if all is well. Remember me to your father and mother and brother. I was on this Parade by the King. Remember me to all.

King George V regularly inspected British, Australian and Canadian troops on Salisbury Plain. The postcard below is from one such inspection.

His Majesty the King inspects troops on Salisbury Plain.

As well as the military camps, soldiers were also billeted in civilian houses all over Britain. Frank was sent with his battalion to train in Bishop's Stortford, Hertfordshire. He sent home a postcard with a pre-war view of the town with the following message:

Postmarked Bishop's Stortford, 6 December 1915: Just a line to let you know I have received parcel. I have not had time to open yet but a letter will follow. We have been out marching and skirmishing and shewn fighting night and day since Friday morning. We started at 2am and we are not finished yet. Sleeping out when we can catch a nap. They are putting us through it. I have had no money yet. But I suppose I shall have it sometime. I am in the best of health and getting as hard as nails. I am eating like a horse. Yours forever, Frank

Ethel sent a postcard to her friend with a message about the troops billeted in Streatham, south London. She was not impressed with the behaviour of some of the soldiers from the Royal Engineers with her disapproval clear in her short message.

Postmarked Streatham, south west London 28 April 1916: My dear G, very many thanks for postcard just arrived. Town is getting quite full up with soldiers. We have one billeted with us. Seems the only one in this road so far! Wish you were home to entertain him! He's quite a gentleman and we are very lucky to have such a fellow. Some are – well never mind. They are Royal Engineers. We hope you are fit and pray you may be kept safely. Dad went to Southend with Mr Turner last week-end. Heaps of love and all good wishes. Ethel

In 1915, the 2/8 Battalion of the Worcestershire Regiment were billeted in Essex. The postcard below shows that they had occupied a railway carriage at Tollesbury Pier station and converted it to their own Zeppelin View Hotel. Zeppelins bombed nearby Maldon on 15 April 1915 causing damage to buildings in the town. The only death was that of a chicken. The Worcester's Zeppelin View Hotel was a response to that bombing raid.

Zeppelin View Hotel, 2/8 Worcesters, Tollesbury Pier, Essex 1915.

Many postcards were printed in Britain with rude or insulting caricatures of the Kaiser. Often these postcards were overprinted with the name of a particular regiment, battalion or corps. This made them instantly collectible for soldiers serving within that regiment, and their families. Two such postcards are shown on this page; one overprinted for the Royal Engineers, the other for the Devonshire Regiment.

For gootness sake Halt !
der Royal Engineers
are koming.

Left: Before he left his home town of Falmouth, Stanley Hugh of the Royal Engineers sent this parting postcard to his sister.

Postmarked Falmouth 2 April 1915: Dearest Sis. Just a postcard. So sorry I could not come over. We have been busy today and training and getting ready for the morrow. Came down here about 7:30 but was not allowed to come across by ferry. If I would [have] time I would have come up around Penryn. We are off in the morning about 6:30 train. Goodbye for the time. Will write every chance I get. Best love. Stanley

Below: Postmarked 13 April 1915
A Company, 10th Devons, Syndey Place, Bath: Just a few lines to let you know that I arrived back safe & sound about 11pm. Ta ta for present. Yours etc. Charlie

Charlie of the 10th (Service) Battalion of the Devonshire Regiment was stationed in Bath when he sent home this cartoon of Britain scoring a goal against the Kaiser.

The artist Bruce Bairnsfather was a popular wartime artist of comic postcards. His series 'Fragments from France' was well-liked by soldiers and civilians alike.[1:7]

Postmarked Bootle, Liverpool, 29 September 1916

> Quartermasters' Office, 3rd Garrison, Cheshire Regiment, Irlam Road, Bootle: We have got fairly well settled down in our new quarters. It is a change from the country. Best wishes, Harold

Postmarked Shorncliffe Camp, nr Sandgate, Kent, 24 September 1916

> Dear Hilda, I guess you will be surprised to get this from here. I have been recalled to my regiment. I expect to be home on a couple of days on leave. I guess it won't be long before I'm on the old job again as per picture. Charlie.

Charlie's reference to be 'on the old job again' referred to him returning to active duty fighting in the trenches.

The next postcard was sent from the aerodrome at Hounslow Heath where various squadrons of the Royal Flying Corps were based. The Royal Flying Corps was amalgamated with the Royal Navy Air Service to form the Royal Air Force in April 1918. The unknown sender of this postcard was possibly from the 39 Squadron of the Royal Flying Corps, whose task was to defend Britain from German bombers and air raids.[1:8]

A PORTION OF THE INTERIOR OF CHURCH ARMY HUT-THE CONCERT END

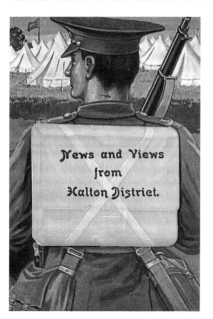

Above: A Portion of the Interior of Church Army Hut, The Concert End CA Hut, Aerodrome, Hounslow Heath, London, 20 October 1917

This is the view of the Concert end of the hut. My bedroom marked X. Platform and piano A and devotional room B. Tell Mary will send her photo of outside of the hut another day. Have not time now as we open in a few minutes & I must look after things. Love to you all. Yours ever, G.B.

Left: An unknown soldier was based at Halton Park, near Tring in Hertfordshire. There is no date on the postcard but the message refers to the zeppelin raid over Tring on the night of 2/3 September 1916. [1:9]

Halton Park Army Camp: Halton Park Army Camp: From Jim to mother and sister. Just a postcard hoping to find you in the best of health as it leaves me the same. The zepps are here at night and we have to hide ourselves in the woods, we get no sleep just lately. Good night.

Bury St Edmunds, 12 September 1915 The Gardens, Sunday afternoon, 12 September 1915. Dear M, hope to return Wednesday evening, 10 to 7 at Loudwater. Had a zep over here again at 1 o'clock this morning, 10 sheep killed. Heard anti-aircraft guns firing at those that were on way to London Thursday evening about 9 o'clock. We do see life! Love to all

ZEPPELIN RAID. BURY St EDMUNDS APRIL 30/15

Real photographic postcards with scenes of the damage caused by the air raids on Britain were common. The above postcard was sent from Bury St Edmunds in Suffolk and shows the damage to shops caused by a zeppelin air raid which took place on the night of 30 April 1915. The message on the back refers to a later raid on the town during the night of 11/12 September 1915.

Newspapers collected money from their readers to purchase Christmas parcels and presents which were sent abroad to servicemen. Picture postcards were sent from the newspapers to these readers, thanking them for their money. The two postcards on the next page were thanking readers for purchasing individual Christmas puddings which were sent to soldiers during the Christmases of 1915 and 1916. The genial, warm and welcoming trenches depicted was a blissful fantasy for people at home, compared to the stark reality of trench warfare.

Chapter 2

Greetings from the Trenches

A few days after Britain's declaration of war on Germany on 4 August 1914, the British Expeditionary Force (the BEF) arrived in France. With the BEF were a number of officers and men from the military postal unit, the Royal Engineers Special Reserve (Postal Section), also known as the Royal Engineers Postal Section (R.E.P.S.). This unit had been setup the previous year in February 1913 by the War Office and was originally staffed by men who had already worked for the General Post Office in Britain.[2:1] This was the start of a massive operation to get letters, postcards and parcels to and from serving men (and female nurses and workers) backwards and forwards between the Western Front and Britain. Postcards immediately became a method for sending quick messages back to loved ones in Britain, with letters used for longer news. All mail sent from the Western Front was censored by junior officers before the item entered the postal system. This was a precaution against any sensitive information falling into enemy hands. Thus soldiers' postcards have messages written in general or vague terms, rarely mentioning locations or towns and villages where they were fighting.

A soldier from an unknown regiment, Bert Clarke, sent postcards home to his parents in Charlton (south-east London) with messages about his conditions in France and acknowledgements of the deaths of family friends. He sailed for France on Wednesday 4 November 1914, aboard the 6,306-ton cargo vessel *The Oxonian* which was used to transport troops to France in 1914. In the postcard below, his first surviving postcard, his handwriting is very shaky and his message is in the past tense – 'we embarked on *The Oxonian*' instead of 'we embark on *The Oxonian*' – yet the postmark is that of Southampton. Therefore, it is likely that he wrote this postcard while waiting on board

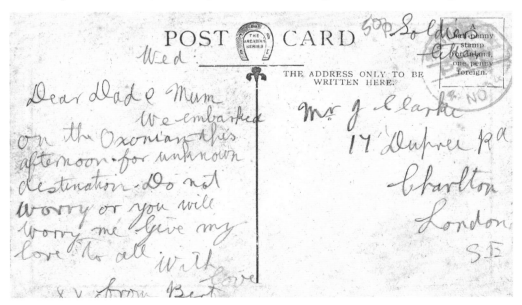

Postmarked Southampton 4 November 1914
Wednesday, Dear Dad & Mum, we embarked on the Oxonian this afternoon for unknown destination. Do not worry or you will worry me. Give my love to all. With love from Bert. xx

the rocking ship and then his postcard was taken ashore with all the other soldiers' mail before the ship set sail for France.[2:2]

Bert continued to send postcards home to his parents in South East London:

> 23 November 1914: Dearest Mum & Dad, just a postcard to let you know that I am well. We have shifted further up and are seeing some awful sights for some of the men are coming out of trenches to where we are to rest. I have had a letter from Ada now I want one from yours. Will write again later. With love from Bert
>
> 25 November 1914: Dearest Dad & Mum, just a postcard to let you know that I received both your letters safely and also the pants. I don't want anything at present but will let you know when I do. I was surprised to hear of Will Pope but I was not surprised to hear about Kenny [deaths of family friends]. We heard all about Lord Roberts in fact we were not far away from where he died but we have shifted since. I hope Cec is getting on alright I will write him if he stays at Maresfield [army camp in East Sussex]. The weather is not quite so cold out here now as it has thawed and I am jolly glad it has, it will be better for those in the trenches. Now I will say goodbye as time is short. I will write a letter soon. With fondest love to both Bert xx

Bert's message referred to the death of Lord Roberts (Field Marshal Frederick Sleigh Roberts) who was a general with the British Army and had an illustrious career before the First World War. He died on 14 November 1914, aged eighty-two, at St Omer in France where he was reviewing Indian troops. His body was taken back to Britain to lie in state at Westminster Hall and he received a state funeral at St Paul's Cathedral.[2:3] Bert's reference to Lord Robert's death demonstrates that in November 1914, Bert's unknown regiment was near the French town of St Omer.

Soldiers in France and Belgium did not spend all their war in front-line trenches; much of their time was spent in military camps or support/reserve trenches, before marching into the front-line trenches.[2:4] As a consequence, many British Army soldiers were in tented military camps or billeted in houses and farms all over the French countryside and also in parts of unoccupied Belgium. As ever, a man writing home could not describe his exact location, but the vagueness of their descriptions give an evocative tone to their messages. Bert Clarke wrote to his mother and father and described his battalion's billet:

> 13 December 1914: Dearest Mum & Dad, once again I sit down to write to you hoping this will find you all well, especially your foot dear mum. I am quite well now, got over my cold. The weather is about the same out here, can't grumble considering the time of year. I hope you will enjoy yourself Xmas. We are billeted in a farmhouse and use the kitchen so we will make it pleasant as possible, if we are here then [for Christmas]. Give my love to A & U if they come up. Goodbye for present. From your ever loving son, Bert xxxxxxxx

By March 1915, Bert had seen five months of warfare in France:

> 20 March 1915: Dear old Dad & Mum, just a postcard to say that I am quite well and that I received your letter safely. Awfully sorry I could not answer before but we have hun [German Army] moving around a lot and I have not had time but I will write as soon as possible. Now I must close. Moving again this morning. I remain your ever loving son Bert xxxxx

Bert's war continued in France throughout 1915, 1916 and 1917. After a brief period of leave home in October 1917, Bert Clarke wrote to his parents in Charlton:

1 November 1917: Dear Dad and Mum, I arrived at the French seaport on Saturday. Alright. Had to stop the night at the rest camp and yesterday till 5:30 and then. We were hung up last night at a large junction but slept in the Y.M.C.A. so we have been alright as regards food. It was rough in the channel but I enjoyed the passage. How is Ada? Let me know and apologise to Miss Mukings for I was supposed to have said goodbye to her that night. Love from Bert xxxxxxx[2:5]

No further postcards have survived from Bert Clarke so it is unknown if he made it home to his parents.

Fred Smith, another soldier in France, wrote a poignant message to his friends in Doncaster about his living conditions:

20 May 1915: Dear Mr and Mrs Cook, how are you all? Still entertaining soldiers? I visited a farm last night behind the trenches and heard the sound of the sweet music of a tin whistle. It came from a stable and in one corner of a stall I found a friend Ostler warbling away some Hungarian Refrain. Weather here been very wet and dirty for a week but today the sun is shining and all are happy again. Am still at the same place but for how long I cannot say. I saw Jones & Knowles last night. Quite well. Balmforth has got a commission like Horwood. Kindest regard & best wishes for holiday by all (about 153) Yours faithfully Fred Smith

Below is the postcard Alex sent home to Dundee detailing the location of where he had purchased his postcards. As the army censor had not scored through the town's name, it can be determined that Alex's location was Saint Adrien, near Rouen, and his postcard bears the Army Post Office postmark from Rouen.

Percy wrote to his sweetheart in Forest Hill, south-east London. His postcard was postmarked from the Army Post Office S.11, which was at the large military base in the town of Étaples.[2:6] While this particular army post office was used by many of the military hospitals within the town, his message confirms that Percy was a soldier based in one of the military camps and he was then sleeping under canvas. During the latter

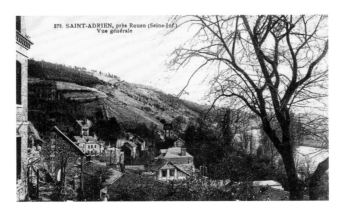

St Adrien nr Rouen, 19 March 1918
Dear Mabel, X denotes house where I purchased the postcards. It stands next to the church. This district takes some beating for beauty! Am feeling quite fit. Weather has broken down somewhat today. Love from Alex

part of the war, the military camps at Étaples became notorious for their tough, often very brutal, conditions.[2:7]

> 6 July 1915: Thanks for the postcard. We are having it rather warm here now, so we appreciate sleeping out with tent well open. With plenty of hard work & loving the simple life we are fit for anything now. Expect you are looking forward to summer holidays. Percy

Arthur sent his friend Frank a heavily censored postcard from the village of Moreuil, in the Department of The Somme.

> 14 June 1916: Dear Frank, just a line in answer to your letter, hoping to find you in the best of health, the same as I am myself. We are having very bad weather and the trenches are nearly as bad as they were back in the winter. As you see we have had our lengthy rest, and once more back into it again. Well Frank, there is not much to write so will close with kindest regards from your sincerest friend Arthur.

Alfred sent his parents a pretty French embroidered silk postcard (below). The identification of the senders or recipients of many such postcards is impossible to discover. The majority of embroidered silk postcards were posted to Britain in envelopes which bore the recipient's name and address. Many of these envelopes were simply thrown away. Alfred used a soldier's typical evasiveness when describing his current location.

> Saturday 13 July 1918: Dear Mother and Father. A few lines to let you know I am feeling in the very best of health. I am now with the battalion in the midst of country scenery & in a little village miles farther behind then where I have been of late. I have received your letter and papers dears for which I thank you very much. The weather is keeping beautiful I am sleeping in a big hut which is comfortable but some are in barns etc. I sincerely hope you are both keeping well & cheerful as I am. So I will wish you Good night & God bless you. With fondest love. Your ever loving son, Alfred. PS Give Marion my love and tell her I will write her tomorrow please dears. Alfred xxxxxxxx

Stan, writing to his family in June 1916, wrote to tell them that he would be going back into the trenches. With no other information on the postcard, it is impossible to discover his location.

16 June 1916
Dear mother and
all at home. Just a
postcard hoping it
will find you will.
I are [sic] pleased
to say. I are quite
well and getting on
alright there is little
news I can tell only
by the time you
get this I will be in
the trenches again.
From your loving
son Stan xxx

The next postcard was written by Fred on Christmas Day 1916. It is a shame that Fred did not write his 'tale of Xmas day in the trenches' on his postcard. The modern-day reader can only guess his story.[2:8]

France,
25 December 1916
The flags we are
willing to sacrifice
our lives for in
order that they may
continue to float
over free peoples.
What a tale I will
have to tell you
all later of a Xmas
day in the trenches.
Fred

As the war progressed, so did the production of topographical postcards of the war damage to French and Belgium areas. Many soldiers sent home postcards of damage to local buildings. William Turner, an officer, wrote to his wife in Clacton, Essex in June 1917. His postcard showed the damage to the town of Rivière, Pas de Calais and the postmark on his postcards demonstrates that he was not too far away in Arras. His messages to his wife are suggestive of his conditions.

RIVIÈRE (P.-de-C.) — Guerre de 1914 - Maison bombardée route de Berles

Shelling Damage at Rivière, Pas de Calais

23 June 1917: We came into the line last night & are likely to be here for 3 days & nights. We had a very quiet time both last night and today. I have not had a single casualty of any kind in my platoon. We are feeding on the same rations as the men and are not starved by any means. It is really a very novel experience. I see the soldiers & officers going up in all directions while everything is as still as death except for vicious rap-rap of the machine guns and the whine and whizzes of the shells overhead. We are very lucky to have had fine weather & the trenches are in very good order. Love to the son & yourself. Yours William

26 June 1917: Still at the same old place & getting along quite nicely. We shall probably be relieved on Thurs night (28th). So that only means another two nights of this job. I am getting your letters alright but you must excuse my not answering them as I have no time really & no writing material except postcards. I met a man today who tells me that [censored] is P.B [Permanent Base]. I will likely get a job in the cookhouse, so you can let mother know. Love to you both. William

George was with his battalion in the ruins of a French Chateau at Evreau in the Department of the Eure. He sent a postcard home to his mother in Manchester.

Postmarked 16 January 1917: Hello Mother, we were camped out in the grounds of this old chateau. Lots of snow and rain, believe me. I'll be glad when the mail catches me up. How is Jim. I hope he is ok. Write soon. Your old son, George

Alf wrote a remarkably upbeat message about going into the trenches to his sweetheart in Middlesborough. He sent her a postcard of a French soldier in their early war uniform of blue and red.

Left: 10 April 1915
Dear R, just a postcard to let you know I am still quite well & waiting to hear from you again. We go up into the trenches tonight so we shall have Sunday in them. I saw Gil this morning, his [sic] is quite well & wishes to be remembered to you. He said it is a holiday in the trenches. Well ta ta for now. With heaps of love. Yours ever. Alf

Below: 12 November 1916
Dear Miss Fossey, have received your letter alright & am glad to know you are all keeping well. I am at present on a bombing course, they keep giving me these things but they are a change so I don't mind. I will write you a letter later. I have not much time just now so you must excuse postcard. Yours very sincerely John J Whitley.

Specialist training of soldiers continued while they served on the Western Front. John J. Whitley of the West Yorkshire Regiment sent a postcard to a friend explaining that he was on a 'bombing course'.

An unknown soldier used an official photograph of the night scene on the British Front, 1 July 1916, to describe how the lights from the rockets, shells and signals were sometimes magnificent.

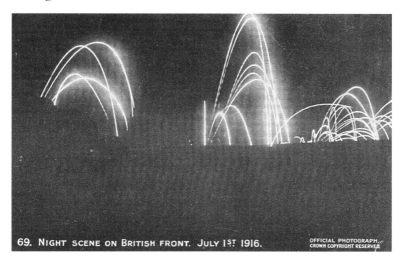

69. NIGHT SCENE ON BRITISH FRONT. JULY 1ST 1916. OFFICIAL PHOTOGRAPH. CROWN COPYRIGHT RESERVED.

These are all different colours and are very beautiful to watch – if you do [from] far enough away.

Fred used his postcard home to teach its recipient about the construction of a trench.

1914-15... Vue d'une tranchée avec guetteur | 1914-15... Vieuw of a trench urth signal
33me Série

France, 30 April 1918
Dearest Ed, Just another picture postcard. I bought this to give you some idea of a trench. This soldier is apparently looking thro a port hole & is on sentry [duty] whilst his pals rest in the dug out on his right. This is not exactly a trench, but a breastwork as the land is too low to dig into the earth because of the water. You will see the soldiers are French. You will also see the rifles to be used. What I mentioned in my letter about moving is up to now partly a rumour, I am glad to say. Best love dearest. Yours ever Fred

Sometimes the despair and horror of war is unmistakable in a man's postcards to his family. Jack sent this postcard home to his sister; his hopelessness and feelings are evident in his message.

Above and below: 14 September 1915

> In the Field. To my dear old sister Annie, I will answer your letters when I get time. I appreciate them very much indeed. You have the knack of writing an interesting and chatty letter & nobody only those who are going through this life of HELL know what it means to hear from home in such a clever way. How I sincerely hope & trust that it will soon all be over, & we get back to our old work & pleasures again. I consider we shall have done all the fighting that will ever be required of this world of ours. Goodbye from old Jack

Right and below: Belgian Front, 28 June 1917

It is impossible to discover what bombardment the sender of this postcard was referring to and if 'Archille' did receive the Belgium Croix de Guerre. However, the paradox of sheer terror and heroism from this soldier is plain to read.

My dearest mummy. It is a damned scheme, my marching orders are not yet here! Tony has passed his examination for motor car driver (Red Cross). We have supported a terrible bombardment, after we were all terrified. Two of our dear boys were killed. We must keep us strong to not cry. Two of my friends and your little observer Archille are proposed for 'Croix de Guerre' on a recommendation and order of the army. You know how much Tony shall be happy and pleased. I shall explain the event when you meet us. I am very nervous because my marching orders are not yet here. I hope! With tons of kisses and my fondest love Grateful little bachelor Archille xxxxxxxxx

"Germany on victory,,

L'ALLEMAGNE "VICTORIEUSE."

— Pas de viande aujourd'hui, mais lisez le communiqué, il est excellent.

No meat to day, but look at the official, it is A.1.

CARTE POSTALE

Correspondance

Adresse

N° 108 — P. J. Gallais et Cie, éditeurs, 38, Rue Vignon. Paris. Visé n° 108.

29

Soldiers serving overseas were eager to hear news from Britain and the Allies. Alma, writing to Ada in Cromer, Norfolk, wrote of the sinking of the passenger ship the RMS *Lusitania* on 7 May 1915 by a German U-Boat. The ship was sailing from New York to Liverpool but was torpedoed as it neared the coast of Ireland. Nearly all the ship's civilian passengers and crew perished in the waters. The ship had sailed from New York with approximately 1,960 passengers and crew. Of that number, 1,193 men, women and children died.[2:9]

14 May 1915: Dear Ada, just a postcard in answer to your letter. Glad to hear you are well as this leaves me in the best of health. We are having lovely weather now and some very hot times. Hope your brothers will never have to go through one half that I have but must live in hope for the best. Sorry to hear the Lusitania being sunk. Best of love from Alma xx

George of the 2/9 Queen Victoria Rifles sent a postcard to Miss Kerney of East Dulwich. He wrote about the air raids which had taken place in October 1917. Zeppelins had bombed Hither Green, Lewisham, in south-east London in raids, killing several people including seven children from the same family.[2:10]

28 October 1917
> Dear Miss Kearney, very sorry that I haven't written before, but I haven't settled anywhere so it wasn't really any use. I am on my way to the line now. Just resting at this place before continuing in [censored] I shall join the 2/9th QVRs [Queen Victoria's Rifles] and will write as soon as settled. I hope you are not affected by the air-raids! Did you receive my postcard from Southampton? That's all for present. Au revoir. Yours sincerely George.

Frederick Sargeant wrote to his father in Leyton, East London about the zeppelin raids which had taken place in the east of England during July and August 1916.[2:11]

France, 8 June 1916
  Hello Dad, hope you are keeping well. Did you get a glimpse of the Zepps during the last raid? Am still keeping ok but wouldn't mind a few days' holiday. Guess you'll miss Winnie for the next week. Best love to mother and yourself Fred

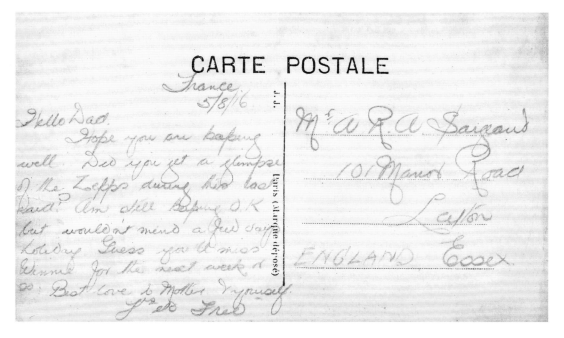

Percy sent his wife a French silk postcard embroidered with the year 1917, and a message that referred to the revolutions in Russia which had taken place that year.

Above: My dearest wife, this is to remind you that this is the year we have to make up and in which I lost my bet. Dam Russia and the whole blooming war. Your loving old mate Percy

Left: Despite the conditions serving on the Western Front, a British Tommy's sense of humour was still very much apparent as witnessed by the picture postcards they sent home. Percy's postcard made light that he had just been fighting in the trenches and was due to go back.

28 June 1918: Hope this will find you in the pink and have had a fine time for your holiday. Received your letter safe will write letter. Just come out of the trenches for 48 hours. Going up again tomorrow night. Love to all from Percy

The next postcard was sent from the Hazebrouck area of France and has the postmark from the Second Army's headquarters. The sender of the postcard, Jack, must have considered himself a 'wag' as his message contains various words of slang along with his own version of French and 'posh' English.

EN GUERRE — ENTRE DEUX ASSAUTS   L.V. C⁰

Above: Postmarked 5 March 1915
Dear Cecily, I received your wee short note today. It was short but sweet. Well old sport, I hope you are in the pink. I prefer the 'Pink Lady'. Comprie? I am at present Nous Old Sport. Does yer heart feel warm tae see Tartan. These are the Bhoys who can do it. 'Always merry & bright'. We got a few here, 'Jocks' they are called. Do you Comprie? Now Old Sport, I must 'ring hoff'. Goodbye just now. With tons of etc. etc., you know. Wishes from Jack xxxxx

Right: Private Edwin Merriman of the 2nd Welsh Regiment sent a postcard to his nephew in Swansea. The 'Square Heads' written in his message was slang for the Germans.

14 August 1915: Dear Alfred, just a line to let you know that I am all wright [sic] so far and hope you are doing well. We have had a bit of bad lucky [sic] lately. Lost a few more men but we will have our own back with the Square Heads yet. From you loving uncle Edwin. Good Night.

If ever you marry a nice young man,
  Don't give it away as a joke
That ever you slept in a sentry box,
  Rolled up in a soldier's cloak !

**Sous la protection
de Tommy.**

Charles Frederick ('Charley') Barnes of the Royal Army Service Corps had been a pre-war driver for a leisure motor-car charabanc which drove between St Osyth's and Clacton in Essex.[2:12] The army put his mechanical and driving skills to use and he became a member of the Mechanical Transport Company which provided transport at Rouen. Throughout the war, he sent home many loving postcards to his wife and children, two of which are below.

30 June 1915: Pte C F Barnes 1275, 316 MT Co Base APO 2 BEF etc.

My Dear Wife, thank you very much for sending me those books, & also my rules. I have just received them. I did not want the carpenters rule but my 1 foot steel rounded at one end. If you have not already sent it dear, do not trouble, I can make do with the small steel one you have sent. Jolly pleased with all you have sent me. Good idea of your making that bag larger. Pleased to hear my little darlings & yourself are now alright. I dare say going back to Clacton has made the difference in you all. I am glad to hear about the other, dear, & you refused. Tell Mr & Mrs Clements I am very sorry if I did not send them a card. I am almost sure I sent one some time ago. I may be mistaken. I have so many to write to that I almost forget who I do send to. Glad the garden looks so lovely as you say. I guess Ms Clements has done a lot to it. I cannot tell you what I mean by something different till I come home.

I have sent my little Ethel a necklet of rosary beads. I hope you receive them alright. I might tell you they cost a little more than Violets [sic]. I am going to buy one for Lena, as I promised her, for the nice letters she writes to me, then I must give up buying presents. I'm thinking as it runs away with a lot of money, & as you know old dear I am still living in hopes of getting a car of our own someday, so must try to save a bit. I was given these cards some time ago at a barber's shop I went to when I was at the other place. He painted them in his spare time, he had got much larger ones hanging up in his shop, they looked really beautiful. I should have like to have bought some only they were too large. I don't know about the S being lucky. I never had much with it as you say. I spent some time didn't I. Never mind dear, if all goes well we must have a nice time when this affair is finished and I get home again. Well fondest love & best wishes to you all. I remain your loving husband, Charley xxxx

After the war, Charley returned home to his wife and achieved his wish to purchase a car, although his business acumen far exceeded his wartime dreams. He established the first motor-coach company in Clacton-on-Sea, Barnes Coaches, which only ceased trading in the 1980s and had a large fleet of motor-coaches still remembered today by many residents of Clacton. Today, the site in Clacton where he ran his post-First World War coach company now contains the offices of Tendring District Council, but Charley is still remembered in name of the council's offices – Barnes House. Below is a postcard of one of the motor-coaches Charley ran in, dating from the 1920s. Charley is the driver of the car.[2:13]

Charley Barnes's wife sent him many parcels with personal items and equipment; including his steel rulers described in his messages above. Many postcards contained messages thanking family and friends for their parcels sent from Britain or messages requests items to be sent to them. In among all the letters and postcards sent from Britain to loved ones overseas were also parcels containing essentials: biscuits, socks, pants, nursing capes, hats, books. The list is endless. Eva Lancaster from Wolverton, Buckinghamshire sent her sweetheart Ernest books and paper. In return, Ernest sent her postcards of French courting couples and pretty flowers.

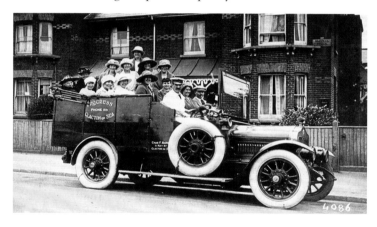

10 October 1916: My dear Eva, just a line to thank you for paper & book received from you on the 8th. I am still waiting for a letter which I hope wouldn't be too long. Remember me to all. I will close. Remaining Yours Ernest
15 January 1917: Dear Eva, just a line to say I received the books which you sent, thanking you for same. Dear Eva glad to see you are getting on with the French. I will write you a letter tomorrow. We have come out of trenches now so will get a chance [to] write back to say how you are. Remember me to all. Yours All Ernest

Some parcels sent from Britain did not meet up to expectations. One soldier wrote about the wrong socks he had been sent. His annoyance and exasperation very revealing that soldiers had to carry their worldly possessions on their backs and therefore did not want unnecessary items.

12 January 1917: Dear Pug, your letter dated 9th. I made a mistake about the socks. My boots are size 7 and the socks therefore will be about 12 I suppose. I want them up to my calves, but not up to my thighs! Now listen. Everything I sent home I did not want. As you ought to know everything I hold I have to carry on my back, so as you may guess, don't want to take more than I can help, so all I need are the socks. I had Katie and Emma's letters. Only one letter from Dorothy Williamson.

In common with countless other women in wartime Britain, Ern's wife in Little Brington, Northamptonshire had taken up a wartime job. He wrote to her loving messages requesting that she used her wages to pay for a photograph of her and their daughter. Ern also wrote of his difficulties obtaining British cigarettes. Many postcards from soldiers contained messages requesting that their loved ones send them British cigarettes.

[Undated message] A lot of riding lately. Well my dear, this is an expensive letter as it costs me 4½d for postcards so what do you think of that. Have you got my watch back again yet and have you sent the cigarettes. I haven't got one and we can't get an English one here but I expect we shall in a day or two. I am smoking my pipe. Yes, my dear, you are having all the fun with Vera but I don't mind so much as long as you are both well and happy. I don't like to hear you grumble about anything but you have been quite good lately and its very comforting for me. So now I must close. With my fondest and finest love and kisses to your dear self and little Vera. Best love to all at home. Ern.

14 June 1918: Just a few lines hoping yourself, Vera and all at home are well. I was very pleased to receive your nice long letter this morning which you wrote at work. Fancy mother going for a week's outing, she never had such times. I wish I was with you to help keep house. I expect Vera will soon be able to do that. I can tell you what to do with your wages, go and have a nice photo taken of yourself and Vera, there's a dear. So close now with all my fondest and finest love and kisses to you, Vera and all at home. Ern

People all over Britain sent parcels to men serving abroad, particularly at Christmas.[2:14] John Bush, a motor-vehicle electrician and driver with the Royal Army Service Corps, sent an anonymous New Year's postcard to Mrs Bass of Snaresbook; his only identification on his postcard was his service number and initials.

050.284. 6 December: Dear Madam,
I have the pleasure of writing to you and thanking you for the parcel which I received. Hoping you will have a Happy Xmas and a Bright New Year. From one in Belgium. J.B.

Many senders of postcards from the Western Front wrote about the weather. To the modern-day reader, the British obsession with the weather can be rather humorous. But the changing seasons and weather conditions, whether that be extreme heat, snow or heavy rain, could adversely affect conditions in the trenches, or in the camps and billets. George, writing home to Chelmsford in Essex, wrote about the wintery weather in France:

26 February 1916: Dear Emmie, many thanks for your letter received safe. Pleased to hear you were all well and glad to say I am the same. We are getting a touch of real winter now – snow nearly 6 inches deep on the ground. Will write letter later. Best wishes to all George.

Frank wrote about the difficulties of getting supplies so he could write letters home:

Quite a warm time of it. I can tell you; was brought down a few miles from here, we hear. We had a beautiful storm again yesterday & I mingled with the Guns, this music & effect was not at all comfy, still one must always look out from some wet apparel in the Country. It's a good job you make yourself satisfied with these postcards, cos I'm thinking it almost impossible to write a letter, as we are so handicapped in the newsvendor line. Best love Frank xxxxx

Frederick Sargeant sent embroidered silk postcards home to his mother in Leyton, East London:

27 June 1916: Hello Mother, still another card for your collection. Do you like these? We are still having rotten weather, showery all the time. Hope all are well. Best love and kisses. Your son, Fred
3 November 1916: Dearest Mother, just another card to put in the album and to let you know I'm ok. The weather here is fierce nothing but rain. I wonder whether it's any better over home? Will be writing to you soon. Best love to all, hoping everyone is well. Your loving son, Fred

An unknown member of the Royal Army Service Corps sent home a French embroidered silk postcard with the Corps' regimental arms.

My dearest Hilda, just a card to let you know that 'all's well'. Had a terrible night (or morning) last night, tremendous thunderstorms, with rain, snow, hail and everything one can imagine. The thunder sounded like big guns at first when I was woke up [sic] about 5am I really thought we be attacked but it sound dawned on me that it was only thunder but it properly shock the house, it has turned out quite nice now (8am) but the wind is very high. Will try & write a letter tonight or tomorrow morning. Fondest love to you dear xxxxx

Even when fighting abroad under enemy fire, sons were still expected to act dutifully towards their parents. Mrs Rogers, whose son Cecil was in France in October 1918, had written to him, scolding him for forgetting her birthday. Her reproachful missive to him has not survived, but his postcard in response, showing a scenic view of pre-war Wimereux, has. He was very apologetic; his message demonstrates that he wrote two almost separate apologies on his postcard. It would seem that the army had lost an earlier letter to her and also he had been ill. But perhaps these were just the lame excuses from a forgetful and neglectful son. Hopefully his mother forgave him and he survived the final fifteen days of war to return home to his family in Plumstead.

39 WIMEREUX. — Le Grand Hôtel et les Planches. — LL.

Wimereux, Saturday 26 October 1918
Please accept my apologies for your 'reprimand' which was very necessary. Is it too late now to wish you very many Happy Returns of the day? France, Saturday 26 October 1918. My dear Ma, I am sorry you have had to send me a 'reminder'. I wrote you a short letter two days ago, have you received it yet? I am feeling much better just now, so perhaps I shall be able to write a more interesting epistle next time during the weekend. Best love. Yours Cecil.

Early in the war, the army introduced the British Field Service Postcard, which were pre-printed postcards whereby the sender of the postcard just had to cross out any information not applicable to him. These proved to be very popular and a means to quickly get a message home. Although sparse with its information, at least family and friends could be reassured that a soldier was still alive.

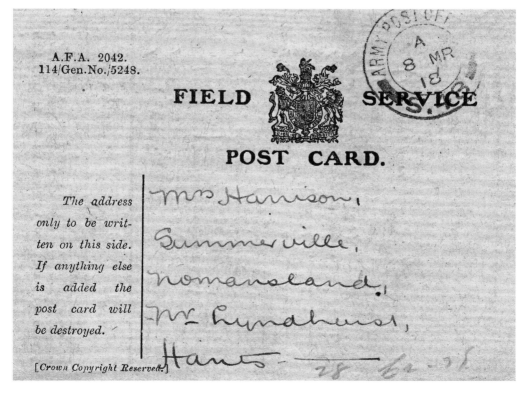

On this postcard, Jack Swift ignored the stern warning that 'NOTHING is to be written on this side except the date and signature of sender' to wish his family a Merry Christmas. As the postcard bears a Army Post Office postmark, it would appear that the post office allowed his postcard through to Westerham – perhaps because it was Christmas.

Chapter 3
The Nurses' Story

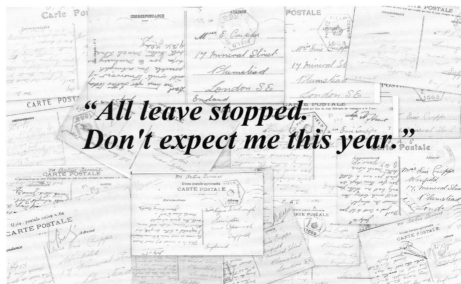

"All leave stopped. Don't expect me this year."

It was not just men who served for King and Country during the First World War. Female nurses and volunteers nursed and assisted within hospitals in Britain. These women often put their own life in danger to attend seriously injured and sick men who had been brought in from various battles via field ambulances and ambulance trains. This next selection of postcards tells the remarkable story of two such British Red Cross Voluntary Aid Detachment women, Clara Emily Mary Woolnough and Gertrude Emma Unwin. Both women cared for injured men wounded during the Battles of the Somme in 1916 in a hospital based at the French seaside resort of Hardelot in the Pas de Calais department. Their story is told through the eyes of Clara and the postcards she sent home to her family and friends in England.

Clara (born 1890) was from the rural village of Levington in Suffolk. Clara's family lived at Levington village's post office, where her family had been the postmasters and postmistresses since the 1840s. It was to Levington that Clara sent many postcards home to her mother and her cousin, Peg Woolnough (also known as Maggie). She also wrote to a family friend, Evie Cripps (also known as Evelyn) who lived in Plumstead, South London. Evie and her brother Richard's mother had been born in Levington, and as children they had spent many holidays in the 1890s and 1900s with their maternal grandmother who lived in one of Levington's almshouses next to Clara's grandmother. The Woolnoughs and Cripps families had been friends for many generations. Clara's fellow VAD, Gertrude Emma Unwin (born 1891), came from the small Suffolk village of Withersfield. The two women met in early 1916 when they were both working as Voluntary Aid Detachments at a small British Red Cross auxiliary hospital in Ipswich.

The Voluntary Aid Detachments was a service founded by the British Red Cross in 1908. The Detachments comprised both men and women who had volunteered and joined units (often local county groups). Members of the service became known as VADs (each initial pronounced individually 'V-A-Ds'), and female VADs were taught practical skills, such as first aid and hygiene, by Red Cross-approved medics. VADs also had to obtain certificates in subjects such as first aid and home nursing. Their duties were not only about nursing; many VADs also had to clean, cook and help wash and dress their patients. Many VADs were upper or middle class young girls who had not been away from home before, and the majority would not previously have had such close contact with men, other than men from their own families.

VAD Display in Lewis Department Store, Birmingham, July 1918
The posters in the window detailed the wide range of duties which were expected from VADs; nursing, working in the kitchens and pantries, housemaids and working in the gardens.

British Red Cross Voluntary Aid Detachments (VADs) on Parade in 1911 at Woodbridge, Suffolk
   This photograph shows a large pre-war parade of the British Red Cross Voluntary Aid
   Detachments of Woodbridge; both male and female units were present. The Lord-Lieutenant
   of Suffolk, Colonel Sir Thomas Courtenay Theydon Warner, is the uniformed man with his
   back to the photographer, inspecting the female detachments. The female officers of each
   detachment are the two women on the end of the lines on the right and the woman with the
   handbag centre-left. These officers are wearing dark red/maroon uniforms which denoted
   their rank. The colour of the other VADs' uniform was blue. A few women throughout each
   line are wearing chains and badges around their necks, indicating that they were trained
   nurses. Each pre-war detachment often had a trained nurse to help with teaching and lectures.

In 1914, the British Red Cross and the Order of St John of Jerusalem (also known
as St John's Ambulance Brigade) joined forces and became known as the Joint War
Committee. Numerous VADs stayed at home in Britain during the war, and were posted
to local auxiliary hospitals to look after injured and sick men who had been sent to
British hospitals. Other VADs were sent abroad to help trained nurses in hospitals. Any
female VAD who volunteered for overseas service had to be more than twenty-three
years old, with at least three months hospital experience.[3:1]

Clara's British Red Cross Service Record shows that she had enrolled in the service
in May 1912 and had pre-war service at the East Suffolk Hospital in Ipswich in that
year. In November 1914, she rejoined the VAD service and nursed at the Broadwater
Hospital, a small auxiliary convalescent hospital in Ipswich, where she stayed until her
posting to France in May 1916.[3:2] Gertrude's Service Record shows that she joined
the same hospital in January 1916 at a salary of £20 per annum. Broadwater auxiliary
hospital was small (just over forty beds) with convalescing and recovering patients
sent to it from the much larger military hospital in Colchester. Their work at this small
country hospital, nursing a few patients in the final stages of their recovery, could not
have prepared either woman for the horrors seen in a colossal military hospital based
in a war zone.

Above: Clara at Broadwater Hospital, Ipswich, dated 24 December 1915. Clara is one of the three nurses standing to the left and centre of the photograph. (Photograph courtesy of the Everson family.)

Right: In 1915, childhood friend Richard Henry ('Dick') Cripps (brother of Evie), then serving somewhere on the Western Front as a gunner with the Machine Gun Corps, sent this mischievous postcard to Clara. (Postcard courtesy of the Everson family.)

1 November 1915: Dear Clara, how are you now? Much better, I hope. Evie tells me that you have not been so well lately. The weather is horrible now & looks like continuing for some time. Are any of your comrades like this? With black hair? Kind regards to all at home. Best love Dick

"An angel in all but power is she!"
"Un ange,—mais une force!"

In May 1916 Clara and Gertrude both volunteered to serve in France. The pair have consecutive identity numbers on the British Red Cross Register of Overseas Volunteers, showing that they had been authorised for overseas service at the same time as each other.

Clara and Gertrude were sent to Number 25 General Hospital in Hardelot, Pas de Calais. The hospital had transferred to the town in December 1915, having moved approximately 10 miles from the village of Camiers (near Étaples) where it had first set up its base in France in the summer of 1915. Before the war, Hardelot had been an extremely fashionable and comfortable seaside resort developed by an Englishman, Sir John Whitley, along with his friend, the architect Louis-Marie Cordonnier. In the 1900s, they had built twenty enormous luxury villas within the town and had added good sporting facilities such as extensive tennis courts, croquet lawns and golf courses. Each villa was sumptuous in its architecture and set in the striking location of forests to one aspect, with sand dunes and the seafront to another. Each villa had its own name, such as Villa Hélène, Villa Edward, Villa Roses, Villa Geisha, and were spread throughout the town. The town also had a comfortable hotel built in much the same architectural style as the villas.[3:3] Prior to the outbreak of war, postcard publishers had extensively photographed the scenic town with its magnificent villas, hotel and picturesque seafront. It was these idyllic pre-war postcards that Clara sent home to her family in Britain.

Previously to December 1915, the Indian Army had used Hardelot for a hospital but this hospital was taken over by the British. On 31 December 1915, Maud McCarthy, the matron-in-chief, and in charge of all the nurses and VADs in France, visited the hospital. She wrote in her war diary that the hospital comprised of the hotel, three villas, four bungalows and two huts. She also found that there were 360 beds allocated to patients in the hotel and the villas. She wrote:

> The arrangements are not good, and there was I felt a great deal too much crowding in the numberless small rooms, as many as possible beds were crammed, with not even room for bedside table to be placed as they might prove useful, a total absence of tables or chairs of any description. The OC [Officer in Command] who went round with me said that the beds should be reduced. In the Villa the same crowding existed. These Villas are quite close to the Hospital. All basements were filled with Hospital stores, as this Hospital was equipped for 1,040 beds. The personnel is [sic] accommodated in top floor of building in Hotel yard (the lower part being set apart for linen, pack and equipment stores) and also in 3 Villas. The Huts are airy rooms for Company and Kitchens, for Sergeant's Mess and Men. The Nursing Staff at present are put up in an Hotel at some distance from the Hospital until a question about a Villa has been settled, the Medical Staff being already comfortably established in Villas close by.
>
> Matron-in-Chief's War Diary, 31 December 1915.[3:4]

In the War Diary of the hospital, its commanding officer, Colonel Robert James Copeland (a qualified medical doctor and a member of the Royal Army Medical Corps), wrote each day extensive entries about the daily running of his hospital. He also documented the regular expansion his hospital required to keep up with the demands of the war and its high number of casualties.[3:5] In time, Villas Hélène and Edward were used as wards: Villa Roses was used by nursing staff, and Villa Stugan had an operating theatre and was also used as nurses' quarters. The nursing of sick and wounded men was made more difficult because the villas and the hotel were spread throughout the town of Hardelot.

By February 1916, the hospital consisted of 1,040 fully equipped beds; it also had resources of 4,000 blankets, forty stretchers and 400 mattress-cases. The same month, the hospital was required to expand to 1,600 beds. The colonel calculated that the expansion could be accommodated with 375 beds in the existing villas, forty in the mess's dining hut, 700 in existing hospital marques/tents, and the remaining beds accommodated in a further thirty-five new hospital marques. In addition to the extra beds and marques, the colonel also calculated that he needed more lighting and water provision, a cooking shed, and additional latrine facilities, an incinerator, material for paths, an ablution room, and an extra lorry for rations and supplies. He also documented that the pre-extension nursing staff comprised of nineteen nurses and seven VADs, but he required thirty nurses and thirty-nine VADs. He also specified that he required an additional number of nurses 'for emergency', calculated at three trained nurses and two VADs for each hundred beds. This vast expansion took time.

In March 1916, the Colonel documented that by this time there were fifty-two large hospital marques, along with eighteen bell tents. The matron-in-chief visited the hospital in April 1916 and found that there were

> …two villas where patients are admitted, also [I visited] to marques where Hospital is expanding. Every arrangement good, mainly mild cases. On each a room has been set apart as a dressing room, where all up patients can be dressed. Nursing Staff accommodated in two Villas, arrangements very good. Two more Villas have been selected. When sanction is obtained the Staff can be increased from 29 to 86 to complete Staff. Hospital now equipped for 1,050 beds and expanding to 1,500. The [Nursing] Home is well run by Mrs. Burdon, Home Sister.
>
> Matron-in-Chief's War Diary, 13 April 1916.

By May 1916, in addition to the wards in the villas, the hospital comprised seventy-nine hospital marquees (fifty with wooden flooring and the rest with tarpaulin flooring), and twenty-six scullery tents. The matron-in-chief reported that a third villa had been taken in the town, so that a staff of seventy-three trained nurses and VADs could be accommodated. By 30 June 1916, the eve of the Battles of the Somme, the hospital finally had the number of beds the colonel had calculated he required in March. By June, the hospital comprised of eighty-seven hospital marquees for 1,218 cases, with fourteen beds in each marque. Beds were also available in the bell tents and villas, bringing the total number of available beds up to 1,568. As part of this expansion, ominously Villa Mousme had been refitted and was in its new role as an operating room with two tables.

In the months leading up to the summer offensive in the Somme region, the hospital's colonel had clearly been warned about potential high casualties about to arrive at his hospital. It was to this ever-expanding hospital, located just 70 miles from the front-line in France, that Clara and Gertrude arrived. The earliest postcard that has survived from Clara's time at Hardelot was a pre-war view of town posted to her friend Evie. The picture on the front of this postcard demonstrates the idyllic setting of the hospital; in the far-background of the photograph are some of the large villas requisitioned by the hospital, and in the foreground, the pretty beach with its sand-dunes. Clara's message to her friend was correcting Evie's assumption that Clara was to be addressed as 'Nursing Sister'. It was standard practise for a VAD to be known simply as 'Miss'; 'Sister' was the titled reserved for qualified nurses.

In the second postcard on this page, also addressed to Evie, Clara identified two villas within the town to show which Villas were billets.

Despite the War Diary documenting that June 1916 was the height of the hospital's expansion, with new marques and tents being built all around them, life carried on in the

Hardelot-Plage, Pas de Calais
6 June 1916. 25th General. Darl, was delighted with letter last night, will answer it today. No don't put N.S. [Nursing Sister] just Miss please. Do hope you are feeling better today do take [care] of yourself. I'm alright. We're having rotten weather. Much love to all. Your own Darl.

Hardelot, Pas de Calais; the View of the Villas Around the Tennis Court
9 June 1916. The O is where Unwin is and the X is where I'm sleeping. Yours Darl.

same manner for Clara and Gertrude. They continued to work long exhausting hours in the hospital, but were able to take a half-day off each week and a full day once a month. During their time off, the VADs and nurses could walk into the town or forest. An Australian Matron, A. M. Kellett, writing about the hospital in 1917, stated that

> Though a little isolated, [the hospital] is in a most picturesque spot. The sea on one side, with its wonderful beach, where the patients congregated daily in hundreds, and the forest on the other side. The forest was a great source of pleasure to the Sisters, as it supplied the flowers to beautify their wards. Daffodils, primroses, oxslips, violets, blue-bells, King-cups, poppies, cornflowers, daisies, and numerous other flowers growing in great profusion, in the Spring and Summer, and various coloured berries, and tinted leaves in the Autumn.[3:6]

It was during her half-day trips into the town that Clara probably bought books of postcards showing an enchanting and delightful pre-war Hardelot. No doubt these charming postcards partially reassured Clara's worried family and friends back in Britain.

Taking tea on the lawn of Pré Catelan, Hardelot-Plage

> To Evie Cripps. 20 June 1916. Darl, many thanks for letter tonight: so glad to hear you are alright. Will write a letter tomorrow. I expect Unwin & I shall go to town as it's our half day. Am quite alright Darl. Much love Your own Darl. PS Had tea there the other day it's a mile and half from hospital.

Clara's and Gertrude's seemingly peaceful introduction to the hospital came to a swift end shortly after they arrived in France with the commencement of the Battles of the Somme. In December 1915, commitments were made between the French and the British to launch a joint offensive against the German Army within the Western Front. In February 1916, after much discussion between the leaders of the French and British Armies, the location of this joint strike was agreed to be an area astride the River Somme. However, Germany's devastating attack on the French Army at Verdun in February 1916 diverted crucial French troops away from the Somme. Finally, on the 5 June, British orders were issued to artillery units with the date of the 29 June as the day the infantry would attack enemy lines.

On Saturday the 24 June 1916, the British Army started the preliminary heavy bombardment of German lines and commenced wire-cutting activities. During the following days there was the continuation of the bombardment and shellfire, and the British released gas and smoke into enemy trenches. The day before the infantry were due to attack, it was postponed due to bad weather, which had caused trenches and guns to become waterlogged. There was also uncertainty over the effects and success of the previous days' heavy bombardment. On the 28 June, a new date was selected for the infantry's attack – 1 July 1916.[3:7]

On the 29 June, Colonel Copeland wrote in Number 25 General Hospital's War Diary 'all leave stopped'. On the 30 June he wrote 'Sent in names of 88 Non-Commissioned Officers and men under 26 years of age who are fit for service in combatant units, and 6 unfit.' These two diary notes signal that the colonel was aware of two facts: there was to be an imminent attack (with the resulting high casualties), and that the British required as many fit men as possible to report for active duty. The colonel also noted on the 30 June that the hospital's rapid expansion had caused many problems with equipment: 'A great delay in equipping the wards has been due to the pattern of bedstead supplied in which the wire mattress is detached and wrapped in a sack. These wire mattresses have become entangled and have in large numbers lost bits of wire and these take hours to fix up. They are also 6 inches wider than the standard pattern and take up more room than is necessary for good nursing.'

Despite this gloomy portent, Clara continued to send postcards to her friend Evie in Plumstead and family in Levington throughout June. The news of the imminent offensive seemingly not to have been filtered through to the nursing staff and VADs. Or, if it had, Clara was not going to let on or risk being censored in her messages home. Even by the 27 June, just days before the infantry attack, she wrote home that there was no news to report.

The Sun Setting Over the Sea at Hardelot-Plage
    To Evie Cripps in Plumstead: 22 June 1916. Am quite alright the weather is much better now. Am working much. Love you. God bless you. Your own Darl
    To Peg Woolnough in Levington: 22 June 1916. Hat arrived alright last night. Am writing you today. Much love to all. Yours Babs
    To Evie Cripps: 27 June 1916. I do hope you are feeling better. I've got a cold worst luck. No other news. Writing you tomorrow. God bless you. Your Darl

On Saturday 1 July 1916, the infantry of the Allied Army finally attacked Germany's Second Army along a 15–20-mile area around the River Somme, some 7 miles away from Number 25 General Hospital. The offensive lasted from July until November 1916 with a series of battles and attacks in the area of the River Somme. Immediately, the collective battles became known as the Battle(s) of the Somme. Even though Clara's hospital was some miles away from the battlegrounds, conveys of injured men started to arrive via ambulance trains during the afternoon and evening of the 30 June. These men had been injured in the previous days' heavy shelling; bombardment and wire-cutting activities of the area prior to the commencement of the infantry attack on the 1 July. Sixty-seven injured men arrived at 4:15 p.m. at Number 25 General Hospital on the afternoon of 30 June, with a further nineteen men brought in on an ambulance train at 11 p.m.

This was just the beginning of the hospital's involvement with the treatment of the injured and wounded of the Somme. At 6 p.m. on the 1 July, 100 new cases arrived, and on the next day forty-four men were evacuated to England at 5:30 p.m. and a further fifty-two injured men arrived at the hospital at 10:15 p.m. the same night. Throughout July 1916, Colonel Copeland's War Diary is full of daily arrivals of conveys of injured men arriving on ambulance trains and field ambulances. He also documented the total number of men well enough to be evacuated to England to continue their recuperation or be returned back to active service in France.

On 8 July, the colonel started to make plans to once more expand the hospital. This time the requirement was to expand to 2,300 beds; over 700 beds more than its pre-Battles of the Somme size. Once again, more hospital marquees and bell tents were acquired and constructed throughout Hardelot. To give a current comparison of the sheer scale of Hardelot's hospital, at the time of writing this book, the university and teaching hospital of Addenbrookes in Cambridge contains 1,000 beds. Hardelot's wartime hospital had to plan an immediate expansion with more than double the number of beds that are in this modern-day large university hospital.

In total, 3,155 injured men from all over the world were brought into the hospital from the 'front' during July 1916. The highest days' causalities being the 10 July when 245 men were admitted (and 357 evacuated to Britain) and 21 July with a further 345 admissions. July's monthly total compares to seventy-five injured men who had arrived by ambulance train in April (before the Battles of the Somme), and 912 men in June and 1,133 in August. The June total included many men who had been seriously injured during the heavy bombardment of enemy lines in the week's run-up to the 1 July. During July, the total number of men discharged back to active duty was 642 men and a further 1,075 were sent to Britain. The average stay was 6.49 days at the hospital. Extraordinarily, only one man died during the entire month of July. Private James Malachi Oxenham of the Australian Infantry died of gunshot wounds to his head at 8.55 a.m. on 25 July, sustained during the Battle of Fromelles, and was buried on the 26 July at Neufchapel-Hardelot churchyard. From this single death, it can be assumed that many men were so gravely injured during the first month of the Battles of the Somme, that they did not make it to the relative safety of Hardelot and Number 25 General Hospital. They died during battle, on the battlefields, or at the dressing or casualty clearing stations, or died on their way to hospital. Moreover it is likeley that those with more serious life-threatening wounds were not sent to Hardelot.

Receiving casualties into the hospital was a substantial task of logistics and organisation. In his monthly totals of casualties prior to July, the colonel wrote the number of incoming casualties under the heading of 'Ambulance Trains'. During the Battles of the Somme, he wrote his casualty totals under the catch-all heading 'Front'. This indicates that it was not just the ambulance trains who were bringing in the Somme's casualties, but injured men were probably also brought directly to the hospital via field motor-ambulances.

Clara's postcards home stop between 28 June and 5 July. Her first postcard during the Battles of the Somme was to Evie, in Plumstead on 5 July. Her message was short and brief, with no detail about the daily horrors she witnessed in the hospital.

5 July 1916. No time for letter. I'm quite alright; I do hope you and mumsey are both feeling better. The weather has improved this last few days, will try and write tomorrow. Much love Darl. God bless you all. Your Darl.

The conditions under which Clara and Gertrude nursed were atrocious, not just the sheer quantity of wounded men, but also the hospital's basic facilities. The colonel noted on 3 July 1916: 'The provision of hot water for baths having become difficult, write urgent letter to A.D [assistant director] of works to hasten installation of the boiler promised last month. On 10 July, he wrote 'Six hundred and eighty-seven patients fed in the Dining Tent. [These being walking patients, the other patients being too ill to be moved from their beds.] Great difficulty experienced in keeping pace with the clothing and equipment of men discharged to Base Details or transferred to Convalescent Camp.' The influx of men also caused tremendous problems with cooking facilities, resulting in zinc baths being used for cooking potatoes and vegetables.

Clara wrote nothing in her postcards home about the difficulties she faced tending and nursing the injured men at the hospital. Instead, she focused on positive news to tell her family, without referring to her work. She continued to send home pre-war photographs of pretty Hardelot. However, by this time the town would have been churned up with the mechanics and manoeuvres of a vast military field hospital coping under extreme war conditions. Her cheerful messages home are in stark contrast to the reality she endured every day at the hospital. Clara must have written these brief messages during her off-duty hours while sitting in the VAD's mess or while sitting on her bed.

The Lake, Taken From the Hotel
18 July 1916, To Evie Cripps: Darl. This is a view we get from the hospital, it's all white sand. This has been a lovely day tho cold for the time of year. Do hope mumsey is feeling better. We are hoping to get half a day tomorrow. Many thanks your letter last night: God bless you all, much love. Your own Darl

Villas Yvonne and Nelly, Hardelot-Plage

18 July 1916, To Peg Woolnough: This is a view of our mess. The cross is over mine and Unwin's window. I expected a letter tonight, but it didn't come. Hope all are well. I'm quite alright. Much love to all. Your loving Babs

22 July 1916, To Evie Cripps: Darl – no time for letter today will write tomorrow if possible. I'm alright. Hope you & mumsey are both better. Much love. God bless you. Your own Darl.

Throughout July 1916, conditions worsened at the hospital when an outbreak of diarrhoea spread throughout the hospital. The outbreak started on the 18 July when a few cases were noted by the hospital's colonel, and rose to its peak ten days later when the colonel recorded that 41 per cent of patients had suffered from the illness. The illness tailed off so that by 31 July only 7 per cent of patients were suffering. Remarkably, the nursing staff (consisting of seventeen women) had reported only three cases and four cases were recorded among the remaining personnel of 185 men. Infection control to contain the outbreak had been meticulous at the hospital; this form of contagious illness was taken extremely seriously. Despite coping with the huge influx of wounded men from the Battles of the Somme, the hospital put into action a wide range of infection-control measures. The cause of the outbreak was also investigated, but the colonel could find no signs of water or food contamination.

As part of the colonel's monthly report for July 1916, he tabulated the number of men in the hospital and the number of cases, with the percentage of men who had caught the diarrhoea bug.

Date (July)	No. Patients	No. Cases	%
21	1,219	36	2.98
22	1,247	54	4.33
23	1,190	78	6.55
24	1,176	99	8.42
25	1,064	113	10.62
26	980	137	13.98
27	872	107	12.27
28	871	361	41.44
29	825	242	29.33
30	817	125	15.30
31	772	45	5.83

The colonel consulted by telephone and wrote to the sanitary officer, Captain Montgomery Du Bois Ferguson of the Royal Army Medical Corps, for his advice on containing the outbreak. Captain Ferguson replied on the 23 July that the hospital should do the following:

• All water used for drinking, cooking, washing up, feeding utensils to be boiled before use.
• All dish clothes and scrubbing brushes to be called in systematically to be boiled before re-issue and replaced where necessary.
• All sand used in cleaning cooking utensils to be selected from an uninfected area and baked before use.
• Any cooks, washer ups, or mess waiters who have had diarrhoea during or recently before the present outbreak to be excluded from these duties.
• Walking patients not to be allowed to wash up their own plates and other feeding utensils.

Captain Ferguson visited the hospital daily between 23 and 25 July, and on the 26 July wrote again to the colonel, that he was

> Recommending the construction of a new building to take the place of the present cookhouse, meat and food stores, and to afford proper accommodation for washing up cooking and feeding utensils. I have requested that the A.D.W. [Assistant Director of Works] to at once alter the overflow pipe from the water tank so that it shall discharge into the open air. I have asked that two latrines shall have concrete floors installed, and be altered to take deep latrine buckets. Colonel Beveridge considers that zinc baths should not be used to make puddings, or for other cooking purposes.

Colonel Copeland also issued strict rules to all patients and staff that they were not to buy food from roadside vendors.

These letters to the colonel at Number 25 General Hospital, and his own account regarding July's infection, shows the relentless working conditions that the medical and nursing staff were under. Clara and Gertrude were two young VADs who would have previously led very sheltered lives at home with their parents. They were now thrust into the very mechanics of a bloody and dangerous war. Even their early war-nursing experience in the small auxiliary hospital in Ipswich would not have prepared them for this type of nursing. They would have been among the staff at the hospital who were not only nursing seriously wounded men, but also were putting into place Captain Ferguson's rigorous hygiene measures. On 22 July 1916, the matron-in-chief visited the hospital. After her visit, she wrote

> 1,250 patients at time of visit, accommodated in Hotel, 2 Villas and under canvas. Work heavy, but many walking cases. The arrangements for their Messing most excellent, in marques and managed by 3 VADs and a Corporal – able to sit 250 at a sitting, tablecloths, flowers, bread cut, everything first rate. Staff accommodated in 4 Villas, managed by a Home Sister and 4 VADs, 2 French Servants who come by the day and paid from Mess funds.
>
> Matron-in-Chief's War Diary, 22 July 1916.

In among the trauma of nursing, the hospital and its personnel were also themselves in danger of enemy action. Several times in the War Diary, the colonel noted that heavy shelling could be heard nearby the hospital. On the 16 July 1916, the colonel was given tentative orders to evacuate the hospital. Significantly, this was not written into the War Diary at the time, but written in some months later during the following year when the hospital was ordered once again to be evacuated on 5 April 1917. Neither evacuations took place, but the mere fact that the colonel was told to prepare for evacuating a large military hospital shows that the threat of the hospital being shelled by the enemy was very real. The War Dairy does not account for each evacuation, but the colonel would have taken the orders extremely seriously and made extensive arrangements.

Throughout July, August, September, October and November 1916, Number 25 General Hospital continued to take the injured from the Battles of the Somme. Also sent to the hospital during this period were hundreds of cases of men suffering from gas poisoning. On 6 July, the hospital was instructed to open wards specifically for the treatment and observation of gas poisoning. On one day, 8 July 1916, ninety-one cases of gas poisoning arrived from the 'front'.

Among their endless tasks, the staff and recovering patients did have time off to enjoy the beautiful coast of France, which was a tempting playground during the summer months. Unfortunately, not all the trips to the beach were successful. The war diary notes that on the 2 August 1916, two nursing staff, sisters Priestley and Robinson, nearly drowned while swimming, and their injuries so severe that two days later they had to be sent to Number 14 General Hospital at Wimereux for treatment. On 23 August at 6 p.m. in the evening, two lieutenants, Bertram Nobel and Faulkner, got into difficulties when swimming in the sea with two lady friends:

Several men stripped and went in to the rescue. Lieutenant Faulkner was found got ashore and after treatment was returned & admitted to hospital. The two ladies were also rescued – one recovered quickly – but the other had to be admitted to hospital (at the nurses' mess). Lieutenant Noble could not be found.

Two hours later at 8 p.m.:

Lieutenant Noble's body seen in the water – being brought in by the tide. Several men stripped and brought the body ashore. The body was returned to hospital where artificial respiration carried on for 2 hours – without result.

The funeral of the drowned Lieutenant Noble of the Lancashire Fusiliers was held at 2 p.m. on 26 August at the nearby churchyard at Neufchatel-Hardelot.

Bringing some excitement to staff and patients was the arrival of an aeroplane on the beach. On 7 September 1916, Flight Sub-Lieutenant H. Parson of the Royal Navy Air Service became lost on his way back to England, and his aeroplane ran out of fuel. He landed his plane on the beach near to the hospital. The sight of him and his aeroplane caused great excitement at the hospital. Parson was given over-night accommodation at the hospital while he awaited help from Aviation Depot in Boulogne.

Personal tragedy struck Evie Cripps' family when her brother, Richard Henry 'Dick' Cripps, a gunner of the Machine Gun Corps, was killed in action on 25 September 1916, aged twenty-two. None of the postcards from her friend Clara mentioned Dick's death, but it is likely that they wrote about Evie's terrible loss in their letters to each other. It must have been devastating for both families; the Cripps and the Woolnoughs had been life-long childhood friends and had grown up together in Victorian and Edwardian rural Suffolk.[3:8]

From September 1916 onwards, Number 25 General Hospital's main category of patient was skin cases. By the 5 September, 50 per cent of the patients were skin cases and on the 12 September, special wards were opened to deal with just these cases. These cases were sent to the hospital from all over France, before the men were well enough to be either sent to Britain or return to duty. The matron-in-chief visited on the 19 October and inspected two of the villas which were to be converted into wards for officers with skin conditions. She documented that the two villas were side by side and were to contain rooms for the officers, ante-rooms, special bath rooms, kitchens and sculleries, and day rooms. At this trip, she also commented that the sisters had the use of the three gravel tennis courts in Hardelot-Place, although she did not note if the VADs were also allowed to use the courts.

During this time, Clara continued to send her postcards home, and her family sent her parcels containing items of clothing. To her cousin, Clara wrote:

2 October 1916: Dear Peg, Parcel arrived alright. I am afraid 'gowns' won't do. They are not large enough. Will you be able to change them? Am writing you today. Too cold for words. Much love to all, Babs

To her friend Evie Cripps,

21 October 1916: Darl, no time for letter, will try and write tomorrow. Weather too cold for words. I do hope you are all well. Much love, God Bless You, Your own Darl

The winter months brought harsh conditions to the hospitals. Clara's October message 'too cold for words' to her family totally understated her working conditions during the winter of 1916. On 18 November, the colonel wrote in the War Diary:

Write recommending strongly that doors be fitted to the tents [wards] for winter. The only means at present of closing the wards at present is by lacing them up – this renders exit in case of fire & also passage in and out for patients and nursing staff most inconvenient.

Official channels and authority had to be obtained for the much-needed ward doors. Colonel Copeland's frustration at the situation is apparent from his entries in the war diaries. On 26 November, he wrote:

Reply received from Div[isional] Officer RE [Royal Engineers] stating that doors could not be supplied for tents without authority of I.G.C., L of C [Inspector General of Communications, Lines of Communication], which should be applied for. 29 November: Write an urgent memo requesting sanction for trial of 4 doors of canvass in wooden frames for tents, as being lighter & cheaper and more easily made, also pointing out necessity for doors in winter to allow patients and attendants access – also when the doorways are laced up as at present escape in case of fire would be very difficult.

Authority was given on 30 November: 'Letter received stating that the fitting of doors to the plan of Number 4 General Hospital has been sanctioned by I.G.C. L. of C.' Finally, on the 13 December, the long-awaited doors to keep out the harsh winter, which by then had turned to snow, were fitted: 'Doors being made by labour in hospital & fitted to tents'. The War Diaries are silent as to the effect having doors on the ward made; hopefully they were a welcome addition to partially keeping the cruel winter out of the wards at Hardelot.

On the 14 November 1916, the War Diaries note that the wounded from Beaumont Hamel had started to arrive at the hospital. This village was the site of opening attack of the Battle of Ancre, the final attack of the Battles of the Somme. The workload at the hospital once again intensified as the number of patients entering the hospital increased. The colonel must have feared that November would bring the same number of casualties as July. Clara wrote a brief hastily scrawled message home to her mother:

Postmarked 16 November 1916: All leave stopped. Don't expect me this year.

Fortunately, Clara's premonition that she would not return home in 1916 proved to be unfounded. On the 18 November 1916, the Battles of the Somme were over; the Allies' offensive of 1916 were finally at an end. During the period of late June to mid-November 1916, Number 25 General Hospital had received thousands upon thousands of injured men directly from the 'Front' and had returned home many thousands of recuperating men. It is estimated that somewhere in the region of 420,000 to 650,000 men of the Allied armies had been killed or injured during the various attacks and battles which are known as the Battles of the Somme. There were between 450,000 and 630,000 German casualties. The number of casualties was so immense that sources (both at-the-time and modern-day) do not agree on the total number of casualties on each side. Just a small percentage of the vast number of Allied casualties from the Battles of the Somme had passed through the doors of Number 25 General Hospital in Hardelot.

The end of the Battles of the Somme also marked the time for Clara to return home to her family. This was the first time she had returned to England since arriving six months earlier in the weeks before the summer offensive on the Somme.

Ha____ 'T-PLAGE (P.-de-C.). --- Une Partie de la Digue.

H. C.

Pre-war Postcard of Part of the Town of Hardelot 19 November 1916. Darl, leave is opened again. I may be in England now 21st or 22nd will let you know on landings. Much love. Your Darl

This happy postcard announcing her imminent leave, written on the 19 November 1916, was the last postcard Clara sent home from Number 25 General Hospital. Her postcards sent between November 1916 and July 1917 have not survived. After July 1916, her fellow VAD Gertrude Unwin makes no further appearance in Clara's postcards. Gertrude's Service Record shows that at some point Gertrude moved to Number 10 General Hospital in Rouen where she remained until she was discharged from service in April/May 1919. Clara was posted to Number 1 General Hospital in Etretat sometime between November 1916 and July 1917.

Personal tragedy struck Clara's family on 28 April 1917 when her brother, George Edwin Marwen Woolnough of the Second Battalion Suffolk Regiment, was killed in action during the Battle of Arras, aged thirty-two. The son of Levington's postmaster and postmistress and the brother of Clara, George left behind a young wife and two tiny daughters, Eileen and Sylvia. No postcards or letters from Clara from this time survive. Her family must have been distraught and frantic with worry as she too was so near danger at her hospital in France. It is unknown if Clara returned to Britain to comfort her grieving parents and sister-in-law, although probably not as her country still needed her in France.

By July 1917, Clara had been posted to Number 6 General Hospital. Number 6 Stationary was then based in Frévent. Her postcards home from Frévent were no longer idyllic scenes of pre-war France. Now they were photographs of the harsh realities of war, with army vehicles and field ambulances littering the roads. Her underscored plea to her friend Evie to 'Take me?' plaintively echoes from her postcard (seen below).

Clara's final surviving postcard home was to her cousin Peg of Levington regarding an item of clothing, possibly a winter coat, and posted from Number 6 Stationary.

15 October 1917: Many thanks for parcel and letter today I think I like your Pattern best so please fire away. The weather is very cold I shall be glad of it. Should like the leather lining if possible, if not something warm. So glad all are well. I'm quite alright much love to all.

Clara's postcards to her family stop on 15 October 1917; no others are known to have survived the passage of one hundred years. On 22 October 1917, Clara was awarded her II Scarlet Efficiency Stripes. These stripes were blue and worn on her uniform on her upper arm. It was official recognition that she had served at least two years' continuous service in military hospitals (either in Britain or overseas) and was a competent worker.

Clara continued to serve in France for the remainder of the war; at some point after October 1917, she moved to Number 14 General Hospital at Wimereux. In 1918, Clara was one of forty-five female VADs mentioned in General Haig's dispatches, and her name listed in the second supplement to the *London Gazette* of 24 May 1918.[3:9] Members of the British Red Cross Voluntary Aid Detachments were only eligible for inclusion in dispatches as being 'deserving of special attention' from 1918, and then only if the VAD had served two or more consecutive years in France. Clara was recommended by the administrative medical officer of the area for the hospital where she was then serving. The officer passed her name (along with other nurses and VADs in his area) onto the matron-in-chief. The matron-in-chief then submitted the names of all her staff recommended for awards. It was a great honour and a recognition of personal bravery to be mentioned in dispatches and Clara received a letter commemorating her bravery, sent by the War Office and signed by the Secretary of State for War.

Rue de Cercamp, Frévent

31 July 1917. No 6 Stationary. Darl I'm getting your letter every day tho they take five days to come, got one today posted on 26th I wonder where you are going for your holiday. Take me? Hope you both have a good rest. Much love Darl. God Bless You. Your Darl

— Rue de Cercamp.

Postmarked 16 August 1917. No 6. Darl, I got your postcard that you sent from Clacton this morning, I've had no letters from anyone lately so haven't written any. The weather is very showery. Much love to mumsey, God bless you

Clara continued to work as VAD in France until October 1918, after which time, because of ill-health, she returned to England to nurse at the Colchester Military Hospital. She was finally discharged from the service in March 1919 aged twenty-nine years old. For her time in France, she received the British War and Victory medals. From 1920s onwards, Clara's mention in dispatches entitled her to wear an oak-leaf emblem on her Victory medal.

After her nursing service, Clara returned home to Levington and throughout the 1920s ran a poultry farm in her village with two friends. Her family recollect that she had ill health for the rest of her life, caused by her war service. They remember family tales that she had been gassed during the war. These legends possibly derive from her time at Number 25 General Hospital and her nursing of gas-poisoned men from the Battles of the Somme. Clara Woolnough died on the 25 October 1952 aged sixty-two. At the time of her death, she was still living at the Post Office in Levington, Suffolk, which her family had run since 1840. Probate of her effects was granted to her niece, Sylvia, the daughter of her long dead brother George Woolnough.

Peg (Maggie) Woolnough photographed circa 1900. Clara wrote to her cousin, Peg in Levington, Suffolk, throughout the First World War. (Photograph courtesy of Levington and Stratton Hall Village Archive.)

Richard Henry 'Dick' Cripps, killed in action 25 September 1916. Brother of Evie Cripps and Clara's close family friend.

He had been one of the first to enlist, having joined the Duke of Cornwall's Light Infantry on September 4th, 1914, later transferring into the Shropshire Light Infantry and then volunteering for the Motor Machine Gun Service. He left for France in this service after a course in gunnery at Hythe, and arrived there on Christmas Eve, 1914. Apart from two short leaves, Gunner Cripps put in twenty continuous months of service at the Front, and was a veteran of the engagements in 1915 at the 'brickstacks' (at Cuinchy), Neuve Chapelle, Festubert, Richebourg and Loos… His commanding officer wrote that he: "did his work well and was a splendid soldier".[3:10]
(Photograph courtesy of the Everson family.)

Chapter 4

To My Dear Children...

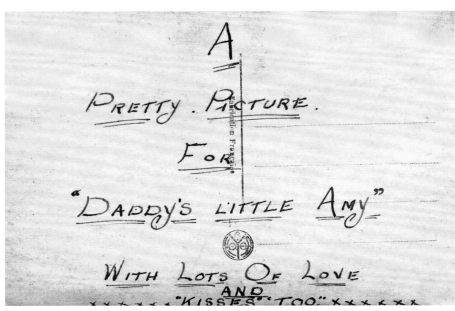

Among the most poignant postcards from the First World War are those sent home by fathers to their children, and from small children in Britain posted to their absent fathers. Often, as these postcards were to very young children, they have only small messages of love between a father and his child, with no items of news. Sergeant Thomas Batch of the 1st Scottish Rifles, was fighting in France when he sent a postcard home to his son Harry on 1 July 1915: 'Dear Harry, just a card with best wishes for a happy birthday and many happy returns of the day with love from Daddy.' Charlie's dad wrote from France to tell his son 'Hope you are well and a good boy.' Olive's daddy wrote to her in Boscombe, Hampshire 'Hoping you will like this pretty postcard. Lots of love and kisses, from Dad.' The pretty pictures on the front of the postcards were more of connection between an absent home-sick father and his child then any message could be. It can only be imagined what was passing through these men's minds when they were writing to their children – children who were growing up without them and whom they might not see again.

Many postcards from fathers do not bear any name or address. These postcards were often sent either within an envelope (long since destroyed) or in a packet along with a letter to their wife. It is therefore impossible to trace many of the senders of postcards between fathers and their children. The fathers' messages vary from just simple greetings of love, to gentle instructions about being good children at home and at school. Internet auction sites are full of highly coloured and beautifully embroidered silk postcards with simple messages such as 'To my dear little Dorothy Margaret from her Daddy.' The father of another Dorothy, but this time from Northumberland, wrote to his daughter from France: 'With heaps of love from Daddie to my little Dorothy and hope you keep well and happy until we meet again.' Amy's daddy sent her a stream of French embroidered silk postcards all written simply on the back 'For dear little Amy'; one of these postcards opens this chapter.[4:1]

To My Dear Daughter
   Dear Babs, just a few flowers for you to paint. Remember me to Lil. I expect you will have started school by now. Goodbye my dear. From Daddy xxxx

Many of these postcards were written immediately before or after fathers had been in battle, and when their thoughts had turned to home. The colourful postcards are in stark contrast to the death, mud and horror of warfare. In the days of the British 'stiff upper lip', it is revealing that a great many of these postcards' messages finish with a row of kisses. Each 'x' representing the ceaseless love and kisses the fathers were trying to send to their beloved children.

To My Dear Children

My dear little sons, I take great pleasure in sending you this card hoping you like it all right. I do hope you are being good little boys and that you are still enjoying yourselves at Aunty Mary's. Your mother says that you are good little boys so I hope you always will be. So this is all at present from your ever loving Dad. Good night.

Until the End

Dear Katie, just a few lines to you hoping that they will find you quite well as it leaves me at present. I thank you very much for the presents so now I must wish you will take notice of the picture and stick to your mother. From your loving Dad xxxxxxxx

The images on this page are the back and front of a single postcard sent home by a father to his little girl, Rhoda. It is easy to imagine Rhoda's daddy spotting this embroidered silk postcard sold by a local French street vendor. He possibly thought that the soldier looked like him, and sent it home to his little girl so she would be reminded of him. One can only hope that Rhoda's daddy made it back home to her.

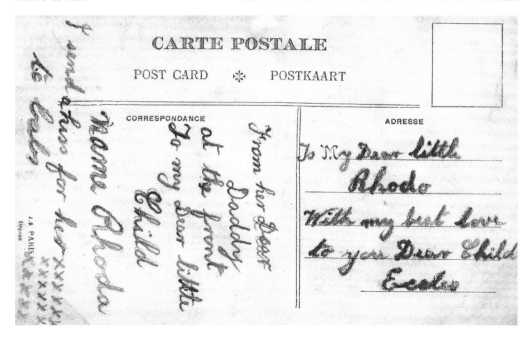

During July and August 1918, Raymond Barton's father sent him a series of postcards with studio portraits of French children. This one is postmarked 19 August 1918.

Dear Sonny, just a postcard hoping it will find you quite well again as you must look after mummy while daddy is away. So make haste and get well. Fondest love from Daddy xxxxxx

The postcards were addressed to Raymond's home at Boston in Lincolnshire. This one is postmarked 26 July 1918.

To Dear Raymond with best love from Daddy xxxxxxx

Maybe the pictures of French children posing in their Sunday best reminded Raymond's daddy of his little boy.

L/Cpl William Arthur Smith of Royal Lancaster Regiment wrote a weekly postcard to his daughter Irene between May 1917 and August 1919. He wrote to his family's home in Hitchin, Hertfordshire, where his wife, mother-in-law and daughter all lived. His messages to Irene (born in 1911) were always in the same format; sending love to her, her mother and her grandmother, and told Irene of the current weather conditions in France. He wrote to her every single week, even though she was only six when he commenced his postcards. These simple weekly messages to her are testimony as to how difficult it was for men to leave their families to fight for King and Country; and how the children must have missed their fathers.

21 November 1917

My Dear Rene, just a postcard hoping you and mother are quite well. I have not had a letter for 3 days. Hope I shall have one tomorrow. Give my love to Grandmother. I hope her cold is better. We are having some rain again. Take care of yourself. Goodbye, with my fondest and best love to Mother and yourself. From your loving Father, Will Smith

18 May 1918

Dear Rene, just a postcard hoping to find you and Mother quite well. I had a letter this evening dated 13th and also the papers. I hope I shall get the parcel and cigarettes tomorrow. Well little girl, I hope you enjoyed yourself last Saturday. I was thinking about you. Give my love to Grandmother. Must say goodbye now, with my fondest love to Mother and yourself. From your loving Father, Will Smith

19 December 1918

Dear Rene, just a postcard thanking you for the cigarettes you sent me. I had the parcel today. Shall try and write a letter tomorrow. I expect you have done schooling now til after Xmas. I hope you will have a good time. I must be done now. Wishing you and Mother a Happy Xmas. From your ever loving Father, Will Smith

24 June 1919

Dear Rene, just a postcard hoping to find you and mother quite well. My cold is a bit better again now. We had had some rain here today, much colder. We have heard today Germany has accepted the Peace terms. I hope it won't be long before I am home now. I must say goodnight now. With my fondest and best love to Mother and yourself. From your ever loving Father, Will Smith

Private George Spargo of the Royal Army Service Corps wrote to his four-year old daughter Margaret at her home in Belmont, Beaumaris on Anglesey Island. He addressed the postcard using her pet name of Megan and filled the width of the postcard with a line of his loving kisses.

VIVE L'ENTENTE CORDIALE!

Vive l'entente Cordiale
> 23 November 1915: B.E.F. My darling
> child, another postcard for you. Hope
> you are better. Daddy is always thinking
> of you. Kisses. Your loving Dad
> xxxxxxxxxxxxxxxxxx

Albert Hughes sent a postcard to his eldest son, Willie, for his fifteenth birthday. The family lived in Llanrwst in North Wales, and Willie's brothers Albert Llewelyn and Hugh Vincent were then aged ten and six respectively. Willie also had four sisters, but Albert's message was for just his eldest boy to look after his younger brothers.

Happy Birthday
> 27 September 1916: Dear Willie, pleased
> to hear you are such a good lad and hope
> you look after Llew and Huw until I return.
> Hope to get a few days leave soon. Dada

To keep in touch with his lad, Frank's dad sent him comic postcards drawn by Fergus Mackain from Mackain's series 'Sketches of Tommy's Life: At the Base'.

Sketches from Tommy's Life

Dear Frank, I guess you would rather clean the knives and forks this way, wouldn't you? Hope you are quite well. Love Dad

Sketches from Tommy's Life

Dear Frank, this is a game which is very popular with the soldiers out here. Hope you are quite well and still keeping your promise to be a good boy. Love Dad

Children all over Britain sent postcards to their fathers. For many fathers, these postcards from home must have been most welcome and a visual display that their children still remembered them. Or at least, if their children were too young to remember them, then their wives had sent postcards on their young children's behalf.

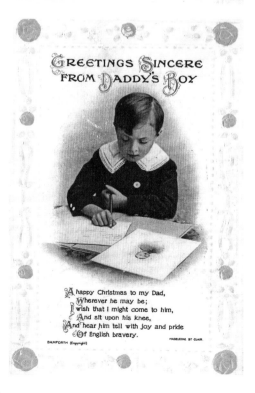

This postcard was sent from Britain to France to an unknown soldier. The message is written in an adult hand.

From the children to daddy. From his loving children.

This postcard is also written in an adult hand.

From Tomy and Jack with best love to my dear daddy.

A PRAYER FOR DADDY
Daddy darling, night and morn
I pray for you, where'er you be –
May God keep you safe from harm
And bring you soon back home to me.

Even very young children wrote postcards to their fathers; their childish handwriting demonstrate their age and the effort taken to write a postcard for their daddy. This postcard was sent to a private in the Royal Defence Corps stationed at Dartford in Kent sometime after March 1916 (when the Corp was established).

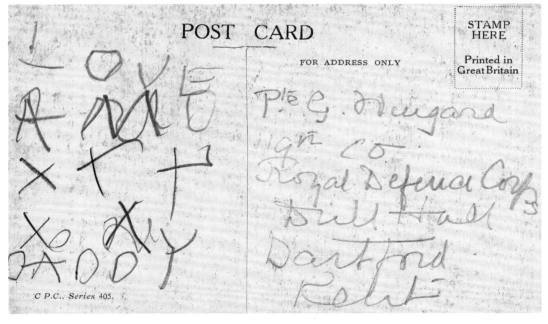

Chapter 5

The War on the Land and in the Air

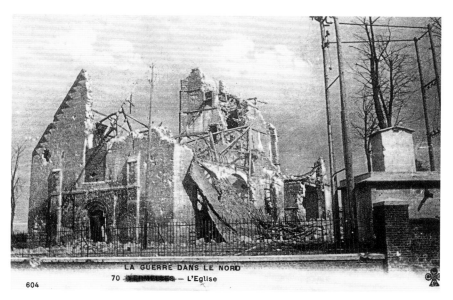

LA GUERRE DANS LE NORD
70 VERMELLES — L'Eglise
604

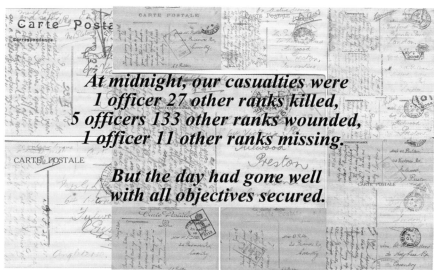

At midnight, our casualties were
1 officer 27 other ranks killed,
5 officers 133 other ranks wounded,
1 officer 11 other ranks missing.

But the day had gone well
with all objectives secured.

This chapter contains a selection of the postcards sent home to Fulwood, Preston, Lancashire by brothers Reginald George Pullen (born 1893) and Charles Edward Pullen (born 1899); both Old Boys of Preston Grammar School.[5:1] Older brother Reg was the first brother to enlist and by March 1915 was on the Western Front serving first with the 1/7th Battalion of the King's Liverpool Regiment, and from April 1917, the 1/5th Battalion of the South Lancashire Regiment. He sent postcards home to his mother, his sisters Winifred and Dorothy, and his brother Charles, who at that time was not yet old enough to enlist and still a schoolboy at Preston Grammar School. When Charles was eighteen, he joined the Royal Flying Corps as a cadet at Northolt in November 1917.[5:2]

The brothers sent postcards home showing views of the towns and villages in France where they were fighting or based. Reg arrived in France in March 1915 with the 1/7th Battalion of the King's Liverpool Regiment but was wounded and hospitalised shortly afterwards. His first postcard in the brothers' collection of postcards were to his sister and mother.

C. V. 458
La Grosse Horloge

Reg's message to his sister Winifred:

26 May 1915: The expeditionary force left the Base on Sunday as I expect you will have seen from the letter posted on that day so I am back again now at the old address. The Battalion is now on rest for how long we do not know – and at a different part of the line. Reg

To his mother:

28 May 1915: Everything all serene here. But I may move shortly but not certain yet. Have no news at present & am not writing until hear from, which will probably be tomorrow. Found on my return that they had kindly presented me with a stripe during my stay in hospital – it was mentioned to me shortly before I got damaged so am now a lance corporal – in the common or vulgar tongue a 'Lance Jack'

The next postcards were sent by Reg to his brother, Charles, then still a school-boy at Preston Grammar School. Charles no doubt eagerly lapped up the heroic tales of his older brother, desperate for the day when he too was old enough to enlist. Reg's first postcard was a view of the Château at Vermelles, which had been destroyed on 30 December 1914. The village of Vermelles fell to the German army in the middle of October 1914, but was recaptured by the French in December 1914. During the Battle of Loos (September 1915), the remains of the Château were used as a dressing station.[5:3] From Reg's message, it can be determined that his battalion was in the village sometime during the summer of 1915.

130. La Grande Guerre 1914-15 — Le Château de ~~Vermelles~~ — Ces ruines furent prise d'assaut par nos troupes, après une lutte héroïque qui dura plusieurs semaines

Château de Vermelles, Pas de Calais

21 July 1915: This was once a very fine chateau but it has been the scene of some terrific fighting so bright moonlight shews off its present style of beauty best. The fighting line is not many hundred yards off in the direction of the arrow, and we were up at this point some weeks back so I know the place quite well. Have been past it at all hours of the night and early morning & probably more often than we should have chosen if it had been left to us. Have no further news of leave but we may possibly come out for a good rest in a week or so and the size of the batches might then be increased. Reg

Two months after Reg was in Vermelles, his battalion marched onto Neuve-Chapelle, about eight miles away. Neuve-Chapelle had been the scene of an intense battle in March 1915 when half the attacking force of the Allies comprised regiments from the Indian Army's infantry. After an intense battle, there were 12,000 British, and 4,200 Indian casualties. Over 1,600 Germans were taken prisoner, and 12,000 killed.[5:4] Reg's postcard to his brother (shown on next page) displays some of the destruction to buildings caused by the Battle of Neuve-Chapelle and a few of the trenches in the vicinity.

By March 1916, Reg's battalion was not far from Arras, in the front-line trenches nearby the village of Wailly and were rotating between days of front-line trench duty and 'resting' nearby. Reg's postcard of the bombardment of Arras (shown on next page) was written during one of those rest days.

Throughout April, May and June 1916, the battalion marched to and from the villages of Wailly and Beaumetz, with periods of several days spent in the trenches at each location. A couple of months after his promotion to the rank of sergeant, Reg wrote to his sister, requesting that she sent him a standard army instructional book. His postcard, a photograph of the damage to the town Arras (shown on page 73), near to his battalion's location at Wailly, and posted during one of his battalion's days in billets in the village. The day of his postcard, the battalion's War Diary recounts that the soldiers had been involved in 'usual working parties and clearing the village'.

33. La Grande Guerre 1914-15

NEUVE CHAPELLE (P. de C.) — *Ces ruines furent prises d'assaut par nos troupes après une lutte héroïque*   A R.

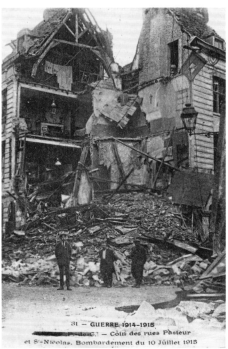

31 — GUERRE 1914-1915

—... P de C.' – Côin des rues Pasteur
et St-Nicolas. Bombardement du 10 Juillet 1915

Neuve Chapelle, Pas de Calais

23 September 1915: I am beginning to wonder whether I have already sent you this view. However it is addressed now. It gives a good idea of the appearance of a well sandbagged trench after bombardment. You can see a rather poor specimen of a dugout on the right – the sort that falls in on your head and buries you if a trench mortar bomb lands on it. It seems to have suffered a little during the general strafe. The latest built dugouts are much bigger and safer. Reg

Bombardment of 10 July 1915, Arras, Pas de Calais

Dated 19 March 1916: This card shews the result of arguing with a shell. A section of a house like that shown is quite a common sight in places near the line – this one is in an important town a few kilometres from our present position. The weather has improved wonderfully it is almost sultry today. Was promoted Sergeant a week ago. Reg

La Guerre 1914-15

Le Beffroi, la veille de sa chûte

vue prise de la rue Saint-Géry

L. C. H. Paris

The day before the fall of the belfry. Arras, Pas de Calais

13 May 1916: Hope you received my letter sent to you at home. When you reply would you send me a couple of 'Platoon Roll Books' published by Gale & Polden Ltd 2 Amen Corner Paternoster Row at sixpence. They are very handy. Love from Reg

Reg's postcards stop between early May and late July 1916. However, the war diary of his battalion, the 1/7 Battalion of the Kings Liverpool Regiment, details that Reg's battalion were in the trenches from early July for over two weeks at Gouy-en-artois, about nine miles to the south of Arras. On Sunday 2 July, the War Diaries noted that they '[had] Divine Service parades and relieved West Kents in Old Section of Trenches [at Gouy-en-artois]'. From the 3 July until 19 July, the 1/7th were in the trenches doing 'usual trench routine'. A total understatement as to the type of 'routine' they were carrying out for seventeen continuous days in atrocious conditions. On 19 July, the battalion was relieved by the 11th Manchesters and they moved into billets. After a night in billets, the battalion moved first to Beaumetz and then to Gézaincourt, a small town close by the war-torn town of Albert.[5:5]

Albert had already been the scene of intense fighting. On 15 January 1915, a shell hit the town's golden statue of the Virgin Mary and Jesus on the top of the Church of Notre-Dame de Brebières. A legend quickly sprung up that if the leaning statue fell, then the war would end. By the time Reg's battalion arrived in the area, Albert was in British hands and the statue was still leaning perilously, but had been secured in that position by the French. From 1 until 13 July 1916, the Battle of Albert (part of the Battle(s) of the Somme) had raged nearby the town.[5:6]

On Sunday 23 July 1916, the 1/7th had 'Divine Service Parade' and Reg took the opportunity of a day of (relative) rest to write a postcard home and described the sights he was witnessing.

The two images below are from a double-width postcard, showing the before and after photographs of shelling damage to Albert's church. Reg wrote on the front of the postcard 'Before and after a dose of our Krupp 'Kultur' pills'.

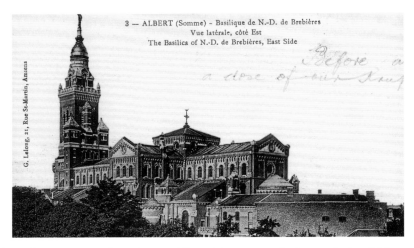

The Basilica of Notre-Dame de Brebières, Albert, The Somme (before and after 15 January 1915)
23 July 1916: Everything all serene. Have been rather busy just lately on the move to a fresh neighbourhood and have had three or four days marching. Hope to be in present quarters for a week. There is a superstition that the war will cease when the overhanging statue falls. Have decided to do my bit in the Big Push by pushing it over at the earliest opportunity. Reg

Reg's next postcard home is brief and not full of his usual detail with his normally excellent grammar failing him in his haste to write to his sister. The few days' respite he had in Gézaincourt, near Albert, was over and he was on the march again. The battalion marched to the town of Candas and then took trains to the town of Méricourt l'Abbé and then marched onto the village of Fricourt, all within the Somme area. Reg's postcard home was probably written by the roadside, in the few minutes' rest given to the soldiers during their march. It is incredible that despite the heavy fighting during the

Battles of the Somme, and with his battalion constantly on the move, the letter he refers to from his sister in Lancashire got through to him a mere five days after it was written. The 'do' referred to his postcard was probably a local event in Britain, such as a concert, staged to raise money for the troops.

Town Hall and Courts, Doullens, The Somme

28 July 1916: Received your letter of the 23rd today. Are still moving [sic] and at the moment marching. Hope the 'do' was a success; are contributions received? Will write as soon as possible. Reg

Reg's postcards between July 1916 and July 1917 have not survived. However, from his battalion's regimental War Diaries, along with Reg's service record, it can be determined Reg's movements during these months. His battalion, by now part of the 55th (West Lancashire) Division of the Second Army, continued to fight in the Somme area of France, and took part in several more attacks and skirmishes within the overall Battles of the Somme. The 1/7th fought a fierce attack on German trenches at Guillemont between 8 and 13 August when thirty-five men from his battalion were killed in action, 113 were injured, ten missing presumed dead, and five suffered shell shock. The following month, the battalion moved to trenches between Delville Wood and High Wood and fought there as part of the tail end of the Battle of Delville Wood. During eight days between 4 and 11 September 1916, nine of the battalion were killed in action, eighty-three were wounded, five were reported as missing and two died of wounds. The battalion also took part in the Battle of Flers-Courcelette (15 to 22 September 1916) at the cost of two men, with sixteen wounded and sixteen missing. During the Battle of Morval in late September 1916, the 1/7th lost forty-three men, 197 wounded, three suffered shell shock and twenty-one men were reported missing.[5:7].

On 28 September, the battalion moved out of the trenches and into billets in the village of Buire-Courcelles. This brought an end to the 1/7th Battalion of the King's Liverpool Regiment's bloody and costly participation in the Battles of the Somme. In total, Reg's battalion had spent forty days and nights fighting in the Battles of the Somme's front-line trenches during the three months from July to September 1916.

In early October 1916, the 1/7th moved from the Somme to the Ypres salient and arrived in the Belgium town on 6 October. Between October and early January 1917, Reg's battalion spent a further thirty-four days in front-line trenches around Ypres. Reg's Christmas Day 1916 was spent in trenches, which, according to the battalion's war diary, by then were 'badly knocked about', and Christmas Day was spent doing the 'usual trench routine'. On 8 January, Reg's battalion marched to the village of Proven near Poperinghe in Belgium to a military camp. From this time onwards, and throughout February and March, the battalion alternated between camp and front-line trenches. Whilse in camp, the battalion was tasked with 'railway construction work' assisted by Royal Engineers.

In April 1917, Reg was commissioned to the rank of second lieutenant and was transferred to the 1/5th Battalion of the South Lancashire Regiment, which was also part of the 55th West Lancashire Division. In June 1917, the 55th West Lancashire Division transferred from the Second Army to the Fifth Army under the command of General Sir Hubert de la Poer Gough. On the 1 July 1917 the 1/5th Battalion of the South Lancashires were at the village of Esquerdes in the north of France and were in rest billets. The village is approximately four miles from the town of Saint Omer. It was probably during this rest period that Reg bought a postcard of Saint Omer's train station, which he sent home to his sister on 5 July 1917. This is the last postcard from Reg which has survived, but in all likelihood it was probably the last postcard Reg sent home from France, as his hard-fought war on the Western Front was nearly over.

SAINT-OMER - La Gare

The train station, Saint Omer
5 July 1917: Am hoping to receive that wonderful snap shortly. My correspondence seems to be badly hung up at Rouen and am still patiently awaiting some things sent from home about a fortnight ago. No news at present. Reg

At the time Reg wrote his postcard on 5 July, the Fifth Army were training for a forthcoming large-scale attack on the enemy. The war diaries for the 1/5th Battalion of the South Lancashire Regiment document that from the 2 to 7 July 1917, while still at Esquerdes, the battalion was 'Training – Tactical exercises, co-operation with air-craft. Brigade Schemes. Practicing the attack in relation to forthcoming operations with tanks, aircraft, machine guns and Trench mortars'.[5:8] Between 10 and 14 July, the preparations for a large coordinated attack from infantry, artillery, aircraft and tanks continued: '10 July: Instructions for Operations' received from Brigade. 10-14 July: Training (Battalion and Brigade) with Special schemes and practice attack (semi-open warfare) carried out daily on Brigade Training Area'. On 20 July, Reg's battalion marched to Saint Omer's train station and embarked on trains at 10 a.m., and at 2 p.m. arrived at Poperinghe (approximately seven miles from Ypres). They then moved into the Belgium town of Ypres and also Goldfish Chateau Camp (near Ypres). For the next ten days, the Fifth Army continued to prepare for battle with 'bombardment by heavies [heavy artillery] proceeded on back areas, also wire cutting and destruction of strong points and trenches; and a harassing fire kept up on enemy's communication.' During this bombardment '[the] enemy sent gas shells into and heavily shelled Ypres. Vlamertinghe also was shelled'.

On the afternoon of 30 July, the army's headquarters moved to Wieltje Dugout, an extremely large dugout built under the village of Wieltje, approximately three miles from the town of Ypres, and very near the Allies' front line. The British and French were now ready for their attack on the enemy. The Battle of Pilckem Ridge, the opening attack of the Third Battle of Ypres, was about to start. At 3.50 a.m. the next morning, 31 July 1917, the First French Army with the British Second and Fifth Armies (including Reg's battalion, the 1/5 Battalion of the South Lancashire Regiment) went into battle.

Wieltje 31 July 3:50am: Attack launched. Battalion was on the right of the Brigade front, with the Liverpool Scottish on its left. Objective, the Black Line. When the men formed up in artillery formation, outside it was very dark and difficult to get the proper direction. This was made much more difficult by the fact that the Battalion on the right advanced left right across and front. There was very little hostile shell fire to interfere with the advance. After crossing the Blue Line and getting extended, the other sections got somewhat mixed but leaders down to Section Commanders showed bravery and skill and reorganised sections as they advanced. After leaving the Blue Line machine gun fire became more and more severe. The enemy had marked spots on which to concentrate such as crossing the Steenbeek [river] and gaps in hedges which were everywhere well [barbed] wired. The advance was made from shell hole to shell hole by Sectional rushes. Support fire was given by Rifles and Lewis guns until within about 200 yards of the objective when machine gun fire from Spree Farm and Capricorn Trench to the north of Spree Farm held our men up. We had the help of two tanks, one of which rushed down the wire in front of Capricorn [Trench] and then dealt with the Trench itself and the other went past Spree Farm and up to Pond Farm, silenced the M.G [machine guns] and enabled the men to reach and take the Trench, which by that time was empty except for two men who were taken in dugouts.

Consolidation was immediately begun but owing to enemy aircraft flying low over the trench giving the position away, it was impossible to carry out the strong ___ where intended. Lewis Guns were sent forward into Capricorn Support on either side up the road and trench was established on both flanks.

Casualties – 2nd Lieutenant S. H. Field [Samuel Hatten Field] was killed whilst leading his platoon. 2nd Lieutenants H. E. R. Silcocks, H. F. Fallan, S. H. Lord, R. G. Pullen, D. W. B. Bamber were wounded during the attack. 2nd Lieutenant J. H. Beach missing and believed to be killed. At midnight, our casualties were 1 officer 27 other ranks killed, 5 officers 133 other ranks wounded, 1 officer 11 other ranks missing. But the day had gone well with all objectives secured.

1/5 Battalion, South Lancashire Regiment War Diary, 31 July 1917

The Battle of Pilckem Ridge raged for three days, although the Third Battle of Ypres continued until November 1917. Known to history as Passchendaele, the battle was fought in atrocious water and mud-logged conditions. Several soldiers drowned in the appalling mud, and many men, horses and machinery were sucked into its terrible quagmire.

On the evening of 2 August 1917, the 1/5 Battalion of the South Lancashires were relieved by Royal Irish Rifles and the battalion moved to the Brigade's Reserve area in the village of Wieltje. The Fifth Army's casualty figures for the three day Battle of Pilckem Ridge were 3,697 killed, and 27,001 injured.[5:9] 2nd-Lt Reginald George Pullen was one of those injured. On 13 August 1917, *The Manchester Evening News* reported that R. G. Pullen had been wounded in action, although no further details were given. On 27 September 1917, *The Edinburgh Gazette* noted that Reginald George Pullen of the 1/5 Battalion of the South Lancashire Regiment had been awarded the Military Cross.[5:10] His citation in the London Gazette on the 8 January 1918 was as follows:-

> For conspicuous gallantry and devotion to duty at a critical moment. He gathered a few men together and rushed them to the exposed flank, where he held up an enemy bombing party single-handed until reinforced by another company and two tanks. He was severely wounded whilst performing this gallant action.[5:11]

The 1/5 Battalion's war diary entry for 31 July 1917 made no note of R. G. Pullen's heroism and that he had been recommended for a Military Cross. But the entry of the attack in the war diary shows that Reg showed considerable bravery during such a large scale coordinated attack which had used infantry, tanks, and aircraft on the enemy's front lines. Reg and his men had crawled from shell hole to shell hole through the thick mud of that terrible battlefield, and he had personally stopped an enemy bombing party. Reg's war was, for the timing being, over and he was evacuated to England for a long period of recovery and recuperation. It is unknown which French and later on, British, hospitals treated Reg.

After the Armistice of 11 November 1918, Reg's war was far from over. As he was once again fit, he returned to active duty and was posted to the 9th Battalion of the East Lancashire Regiment, then in Greece, as a temporary reinforcement officer sent from Britain.[5:12] In October 1918, the 9th East Lancashires had been in the area of the Bulgarian port Dadeagatch (now the Greek port of Alexandroupoli) which was then on the Bulgarian/Turkish border. The Bulgarians surrendered to the Allies on the 29 September 1918 and signed their Armistice of Salonika. The Turks had still to surrender so the 9th East Lancashires were in Dadeagatch as part of the Allies' intention to attack their enemy, Turkey and the Ottoman Empire, from mainland Europe. However, on the 30 October the Ottoman Empire also surrendered and signed their Armistice of Mudros. After the Ottoman Empire's Armistice, the 9th East Lancashires moved to Stavros, on the coast of Greece, about 40 miles east of Salonika (Thessaloniki) and Reg joined them on 25 November 1918. He stayed with the battalion when it marched to Strolongos on the 1 January 1919. The battalion's war diary states that this move was 'for isolation – influenza'. A telling comment in the war diary, indicating that members of the battalion were suffering from the dreaded 1918 flu pandemic and the outbreak was so severe that the entire battalion was isolated. Two weeks later and the battalion was on the move again, this time using trains and motor lorries to get to the town of Sarigol, about eighteen miles from Salonika. Throughout January and February 1919, the war diary lists individuals and groups of men sent to Britain to be discharged from the army. On 14 February 1919, R. G. Pullen left Greece for Britain and was discharged; his long, courageous and hard fought war finally over.[5:13]

Throughout the first three years of the First World War, Reg's brother, Charles Edward Pullen, was a school boy studying at Preston Grammar School. He must have been enthralled by the heroism of his elder brother and longed to reach the age of eighteen so he too could join the forces. Charles (born April 1899) eventually joined the Royal Flying Corps as a cadet at Northolt in late 1917.

In November 1917, still as a cadet, he was promoted to the rank of probationary temporary second lieutenant, and the end of this probation was confirmed on 31 May 1918. In April 1918, Charles graduated from 1 (Observer) School of Aerial Gunnery at Hythe, Kent, after taking and passing his flying officer observer course. After passing his course, on 18 April 1918 he joined number 49 Squadron of the RAF. The RAF was a new force, founded in April 1918, and was the amalgamation of the Royal Flying Corps and the Royal Navy Air Service.

By the 30 April 1918, Charles was in France as an aeroplane observer with his squadron. He sent a postcard home to his sister, Winifred, depicting the Statue of Victory within the French town of Dunkirk with the message 'Everything is getting on alright here'. On 23 May, Charles sent another postcard home informing his sister that he had just been awarded his flying 'wings'.

The Somme and Talence 23 May 1918
I sent you a letter a short time ago. Have you received it? There is no special news beyond my name being sent in for my 'wing'.

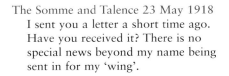

Throughout Charles' time in France, he was an observer in de Havilland 9 aircraft similar to the one shown below. In May 1918, 49 Squadron's air field was at Conteville, Somme in the Picardy region of France, just a few miles away from the village depicted in Charles' postcard Saint Riquier (shown on the next page).

Between April 1918 and July 1919, the 49 Squadron flew Airco De Havilland 9s. In this photograph, the aircraft's observer is sitting in his position in the aeroplane and the pilot standing next to it. The aeroplane was 30.249ft in length, with a wingspan of 45.932ft and a height of 11.319ft. It had a maximum speed of 112 knots.[5:14](- Photograph by kind permission of the 49 Squadron Association)

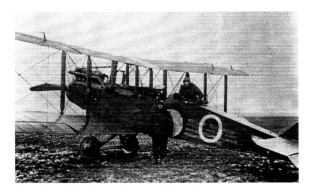

On 2 June 1918, 49 Squadron moved to an airfield at Fourneuil, Verderel-lès-Sauqueuse. A week later, on 9 June 1918, Charles sent another postcard to his sister Dorothy; this time a picture of Beauvais Cathedral in Picardy, with the message 'Thanks for the parcel which arrived on the 7th safely. Weather here is very fine at present.' This is Charles' last surviving postcard home.

The road to Abbeville, Saint Riquier, The Somme, 1918
29 May 1918: Things going on the same as usual here. No special news to give you. This postcard shews a village fairly near us and is typical of the villages in this part of the country.

On the 11 June 1918, Charles was engaged in an aerial battle with the enemy. The report of the dogfight states that Lt R. C. Stokes was the pilot and Second Lieutenant C. E. Pullen was the Observer. At 3 p.m., they were flying their DH9 aeroplane (de Havilland 9) armed with one Vickers gun and one Lewis gun, and were between Tricot and Courcelles bombing at a height of 2,800 feet. Their report of their aerial battle with the enemy states:

[The enemy were] 4 Fflaz Scouts – Two guns firing through propeller. 2 out of control.
    While attacking a two-seater E.A [Enemy Aircraft] between Tricot and Courcelles at about 3,000 feet, which was just below us, 4 Ffalz Scouts dived from out of the clouds on to our tail. Observer [i.e. Charles] fired a whole drum (96 rounds) into the leading E.A. which came within 70 feet, then burst into dense white smoke, fell over and then disappeared into the clouds in a helpless condition. The observer then fired another drum into the second E.A. at about 100 feet, which also burst into a dense cloud of smoke in a similar manner to the first, and also went down helplessly into the clouds. The remaining E.A. did not continue combat.[5:15]

Their DH9 aeroplane was badly damaged in the fight, and they had to make a forced landing in the village of Fouquerolles. According to the case report, their DH9 had its 'main petrol tank, longeron, all main plane's tail fin rudder and propeller shot through during bombing'.[5:16] Both Charles and his pilot returned to duty shortly after this aerial combat.
    Throughout the summer weeks of 1918, 49 Squadron continuously moved from airfield to airfield in the French countryside. By the beginning of August 1918 the squadron was based at an airfield in Beavois, Pas de Calais. On 8 August 1918, the Allies launched a co-ordinated attack on the enemy using artillery, tanks, infantry and aircraft: the Battle of Amiens. 49 Squadron's task during the battle was to bomb key bridges and railways.[5:17] On 9 August 1918, Charles was once more involved in a dogfight with enemy aircraft in the same DH9 aeroplane as the June fight, and again piloted by Lieutenant R C Stokes. This time, both Charles and his pilot were not as lucky as the previous occasion, and their airplane was forced to land with both men injured; Charles seriously.[5:18] As both men were injured, no report exists from either Charles or his pilot. However, there are reports from the pilots and observers of the other aircrafts who were involved. That day, there were two large aerial combats; the first battle was at 6.20 a.m. and another at 5 p.m. (with the same pilots and observers). A report from another pilot and observers describes the type of combat in which Charles had participated. This

report is for the battle which took place at 5 p.m. and was written by pilot Captain Clifford Bowman and his observer Second Lieutenant Philip Terence Holligan:

> [Enemy aircraft were] 20–30 Fokker Biplanes – Tails black and white with blue. As the formation [i.e. 49 squadron] approached Falvy Bridge, E.A. dived on it out of the clouds from the South. Bombs were dropped and formation towards West with E.A. attacking from the rear. After fighting for about 5 minutes an E.A. was observed zooming up under deputy leader's tail. Observer fired a burst of about 50 rounds into E.A. which went down vertically with blue smoke pouring out of the machine. Observer fired about 400 rounds in total.[5:19]

Charles' pilot, Lt Rochfort Clive Stokes, was not seriously wounded and he returned to duty on 16 August 1918. Charles wounds were serious: his Royal Air Force record shows that by the 15 August he was in the Number 8 British Red Cross Hospital in Boulogne and from there he was evacuated to Britain to be admitted into the London Hospital. Charles was on sick leave throughout the rest of the war; his war over because of the injuries sustained on 9 August 1918. He was discharged from the Royal Air Force on 8 April 1919 just two weeks before his twentieth birthday.

The Pullen brothers had two totally different wars. Reg's war was a long and hard one, starting in France in 1915, continuing with countless battles fought within the trenches of the Western Front during the Battles of the Somme and the Third Battle of Ypres, and ending four years later in Salonika in Greece. Charles' war was shorter, just four months from April to August 1918, but just as deadly with his involvement in dogfights in the skies above France. Despite the dangers they had encountered and the injuries they both received, the brothers returned from the First World War. After the war, Reginald George Pullen became a bank clerk with the Midland Bank and Charles Edward Pullen became an Inland Revenue officer with Customs and Excise Department. Reg died in 1973, and Charles died in 1971.

An Airco DH9 aeroplane from the 49 Squadron, with 2nd-Lt S. T. Franks (pilot) and 2nd-Lt J D Hall (observer), comrades of Charles. Photographed between August and October 1918 (Photograph by kind permission of Margaret Dibble via Liz Owens and 49 Squadron Association).

Chapter 6
Hospital Blues

This is where all the fun comes off the best Hospital in I have but England a cross where 5 am,

One of the most enduring pictorial impressions of the First World War are the photographs of wounded and dying men being carried from the muddy battle fields against a backdrop of the scarred and barren landscape. Millions of men from all the services became casualties in what was to become one of the deadliest of conflicts in the last thousand years of history. An injured soldier's physical journey from the place where he sustained his wounds to relative safety in a military hospital was often a long, painful and traumatic process.

Numerous hospitals had to be established in addition to the thousands of front-line medical facilities such as Field Ambulances, Dressing Stations, and Casualty Clearing Stations. These hospitals were established all over the world, in all the theatres of war, and also in Britain.[6:1]

"*Daily Mail*" WAR PICTURES

66. BRINGING IN WOUNDED — AN EARLY MORNING SCENE.

OFFICIAL PHOTOGRAPH,
CROWN COPYRIGHT RESERVED.

The *Daily Mail* printed captions on reverse of postcards, for example:

> Saddest of all, those wounded who can only come on stretchers… some able to move an arm or to look up and smile – they always smile.

WOUNDED TOMMY TO THE PHOTOGRAPHER: "I'M NOT A GERMAN!"
OFFICIAL PHOTOGRAPH. CROWN COPYRIGHT RESERVED

The *Daily Mail* also printed a caption on the reverse of this postcard:

> A wounded Tommy being carried to camp by four German prisoners, suddenly sees the photographer and shouts to him 'Hullo! I'm not a German.'

Pte Eric Perrin of the Honourable Artillery Company was injured and receiving treatment for his wounds in either Number 3 or Number 16 General Hospital at Le Tréport. He wrote an extremely detailed message to his mother who lived in Acton, London. At the time of his injury and hospitalisation, he was twenty-one years old. In his message, he alluded to a common wish by a wounded soldier that his injuries were serious enough for him to be invalided to Britain to recover (a 'Blighty' wound).

View of the town of Le Tréport, Picardy

30 June 1915: Dear Mother, this is rather a nice little view of the village taken from the hill on which the hospital stands. We are of course not allowed down into the village. The patients here are constantly changing, some going to the base, some to England and others come to take their place. Had a temperature last night (99°). Very proud of it and have rigged up a little temperature chart of my own in the ward so that it would appear to be a huge jump up from my previous normal. It amused the doctors. Let's hope it's the beginning of a 'blighty' disease. All the regulars call getting home going to 'blighty'. Heard yesterday (the Chaplain told us) that it's a contraction of the Indian word for England which is pronounced somewhat similar. My woundlet heals not rapidly but at least steadily. Have you seen Jack yet? He is getting 5 days' leave, he tells me, which will mean 3 days clear at home. He deserves it, as does anyone who has been over here over six months. The weather has had a bad relapse. There is strong wind from the S.W. with plenty of attendant rain. Waiting anxiously for the post to come in with letter. I've been having as many as five a day. The other day I had 10, among them were yours forwarded. There were all 10 forwarded as a matter of fact. I'll try and write Katherine Jarvett this week. Letters [have] just come in but nothing from you. Better luck tomorrow. Expected that you will have written over Sunday. Have quite enjoyable Sundays here. There is a very nice service mornings and evenings. Have plenty of friends (many of our own fellows) with whom I promenade along the cliff top. Also been given chewing gum and cigarettes at a beano we had in a Canadian tent in which one of our fellows was. We saw one of our fellows and a Queen Westminster [Rifles] off. They were for Blighty. Love Eric.

Pte Hugh Munro Wilson of the Royal Army Medical Corps was an orderly in the St John's Ambulance Brigade Hospital in Étaples, France. The hospital was established in spring 1915 and was one of approximately twenty British and Canadian military hospitals built next to each other in Étaples. The hospitals were all located next to a large military base which contained regiments from Britain, Canada, New Zealand and Australia. This was a massive army base. It has been estimated that the combined size of the camp along with all the hospitals housed over 100,000 personnel, with the facilities to treat 22,000 patients.[6:2]

The St John's Ambulance Brigade Hospital (whose name was abbreviated to the SJAB Hospital) had over five hundred beds and was the largest voluntary hospital used by the British Expeditionary Force. The War Office came to an agreement with the Order of St John that the latter would supply, equip and maintain a hospital and the former would supply the land in Étaples, along with food and clothes for the patients. The work was intense as the SJAB Hospital received some of the most seriously injured patients from all over the Western Front.[6:3]

Pte Wilson sent a stream of postcards home to his brother and sister-in-law, Ranald and Ida Wilson, in Elloughton, East Yorkshire. Below is a selection of his messages. On all but one of his postcards, he wrote the name of his hospital: SJAB Hospital.

13 July 1916: Dear Ida, here we are again. Have you started on war work yet, I wonder, Eh? It is terribly cold today and miserable, have not like summer at all here. Hughie.

17 July 1916: Dear Ran, many thanks for the [news]paper, I quite enjoyed reading it. I have passed it on to the other boys now. The news has grown more hopeful lately. Much love

26 July 1916: Dear Ran, how are you getting on? Hope you are keeping well and happy like your humble. Am enjoying ward work as [a] treat. Give my love to all including Ida. Hughie

31 December 1916: Dear Ida, many thanks for the biscuits received last night. They're all gone now. They were champion. Only hope there are more to follow. Love Hughie

1 January 1917: Dear Ida, just to wish you a 'Bonne Annee'. What sort of Xmas have you? Give my love to you mother & Ran & heaps for yourself, Hughie.

17 February 1917: Dear Ida, many thanks for your parcel received this afternoon. The biscuits are lovely. Sorry I cannot write a letter to thank you as we are now restricted to two letters a week but I will write you a letter as soon as ever possible. Hope Mrs Dorsey is keeping well despite the cold weather. Much love to Ran and yourself. Hughie

In mid-May 1917, Private Wilson became a patient within his own hospital, the SJAB, for an unknown reason, although more likely to have been sickness rather than injury.

29 May 1917: Dear Ran, many thanks for your letter received this morning. I am pleased to say I am out of hospital but not on full duty again yet and I am feeling better now. Give my love to Ida and Mrs D and also yourself. Your loving brother Hughie

Whatever his illness was, Hugh had recovered by the time of his postcard dated 13 July 1917.

Dear Ida, here we are again still smiling & happy. Had to say I am absolutely fine once more. How are you keeping? Remember me kindly to Mrs Dorsey. Love to Ran and yourself Hughie

On the 17 May 1918, the Germans commenced bombing air raids on the area of Étaples and on the 19 May, the SJAB hospital was bombed. Maud McCarthy, the matron-in-chief wrote in her war diary:

> 19 May, Étaples: A very severe air-raid took place over the hospitals, lasting for 3 hours. No.1 Canadian General Hospital suffered most heavily in personnel, - 1 Nursing Sister being killed, 2 severely wounded (have since died) and 5 others wounded. At No.26 General Hospital there were two minor casualties amongst the nursing staff and the Sisters' quarters were partly wrecked. At No.46 Stationary Hospital there was one casualty – a VAD being slightly wounded. Many patients and personnel were killed and wounded. Nos.35, 37, 2 and 4 Ambulance Trains were lying at Étaples and S/Nurse M. de H. Smith, of 35 AT, was slightly wounded above the eye, by a splinter of glass. All these trains were more or less damaged.[6:4]

Throughout May, the Germans continued to bomb Étaples, and on the 31 May, the SJAB hospital was hit once again. The matron-in-chief wrote:

> 31 May, Étaples: There was a terrible raid right over the hospitals. Practically all the Étaples hospitals suffered, those which had the most casualties being the St. John's Ambulance Brigade hospital, where 1 Sister was killed and 5 wounded, besides many patients and personnel, the Liverpool Merchants' Hospital (1 Sister wounded), No.24 General Hospital (2 of the nursing staff wounded, one severely), No.56 General Hospital, where there were no casualties amongst the nursing staff but the administrative block was almost destroyed, and No.26 General Hospital, as well as the two Canadian hospitals (Nos.1 and 7) which had suffered so severely before. The St. John's Ambulance Brigade Hospital, which was beautifully equipped, is entirely wrecked. Matron-in-Chief's War Diary, 31 May 1918.

This second air-raid attack was so serious that the SJAB hospital was forced to immediately close as so much damaged had been done to its facilities. The bombing of Étaples continued sporadically until the air raids stopped in August 1918. There was an outcry at the time about the nature of the air raids and newspapers throughout Britain were full of the horror and the atrocity of bombing hospitals.[6:5] However, it has been suggested that the German

Le Havre, British Hospital Ship *Asturias*, 1918
Glad to say I am out of hospital once more. My arm is getting on nicely. Love to all at B.V.. [Belle Vue]
Hughie

target was not the hospitals, but rather the nearby railway bridge over the River Canche and the military training bases which were so near to the hospitals.[6:6]

It would seem that orderly Pte Wilson of the SJAB hospital was injured during one of Étaples' air-raids. His final postcard home (shown on the previous page) is the only postcard in the set of his surviving postcards where he did not give his hospital's name. With a blurred postmark, a precise month to this card cannot be given. However, the lack of the name of his hospital and the contents of his message are revealing Pte Wilson's army records have not survived, however it is likely that he received the injury to his arm during the air raids of May 1918. His final surviving postcard home was probably sent from another hospital in Étaples where he had been sent to recuperate from his injuries before he could return to duty.

Many seriously wounded men had to be evacuated back to Britain from the hospitals of the Western Front with ships and trains used to perform this task. There were so many causalities requiring evacuation that entire ships were drafted or requisitioned, and then equipped as floating hospitals. Some of these hospital ships were temporarily moored for lengthy periods in locations within French or Belgian seaports. Whilse the ship was docked in harbour, it was then loaded with the injured. When the hospital ship was full, it returned to Britain with wounded men.

R. G. Cowie was working at Number 2 General Hospital in Le Havre (possibly as an orderly) when he saw docked in the harbour, the hospital ship HMHS *Asturias*. Shortly after R. G. Cowie sent his postcard home to Sunbury in Middlesex, HMHS *Asturias* returned to Avonmouth in Britain with 1,000 men. These men were unloaded at Avonmouth for onward evacuation to British hospitals. On the night of 20/21 March 1917, the empty ship (apart from crew) was making its way from Avonmouth to Southampton when it was torpedoed by a German U-boat and sunk with the loss of over thirty crew, a further number of nearly thirty crew were injured and others declared missing.[6:7] Torpedoing a hospital ship was declared a 'dastardly outrage' by the British press. Newspapers reported that the ship had 'all the proper distinguishing Red Cross signs brilliantly illuminated'.

Le Havre, British Hospital Ship *Asturias*. 7 February 1917: No 2 General Hospital, still here. I have got through a little more of my correspondence. I hope you are keeping fit. My cold is getting better by degrees. This hospital ship is moored in the quay where I live. R. G. Cowie

Once a wounded man had been returned to Britain, he was sent on to a British hospital. Some of these hospitals were the more traditional pre-war general hospitals, while others were the new auxiliary hospitals which had sprung up throughout Britain.

Auxiliary hospitals generally came under the joint operations of the British Red Cross and St John's Ambulance Brigade, who were loaned (or requisitioned) many grand country houses for the duration of the war.[6:8] These houses were converted into military hospitals and convalescence homes for wounded or sick service men. The photograph at the start of this chapter is one such grand house, Gledhow Hall in Leeds, formerly the home of Lord Airedale. It became a Voluntary Aid Detachment (VAD) hospital under the control of St John's Ambulance in May 1915.[6:9]

Another British auxiliary hospital was Dunsdale Red Cross Hospital in Westerham, Kent. In late 1914, it opened its doors as a hospital at Dunsdale House, Brasted Road in Westerham, Kent. The house had been built as a grand country home for a gentleman of significant means and had landscaped gardens in addition to its extensive buildings. In the early years of the war, the hospital took in Belgian soldiers, but by the time of this photograph below, many patients were British soldiers.[6:10] Edith Pearce visited the hospital and sent this postcard to her mother in 1916.

Above: Dunsdale Red Cross Hospital
   Postmarked 16 May 1916: Dear Mum, hope this will find you quite well. Give my love to dad. The weather much colder. These are some of the soldiers we go and see, they are all getting on well. Thank Daisy for letter. Love to all, Edith

Arch's sister sent him a postcard with a stirring poem entitled 'To a Brave One Wounded'.

Dear Arch. Just a card hoping this will find you still progressing and hope that you will soon be home again. We have not heard anything from the Matron yet. Love from your loving sister Lottie.

Ruth went to see her sweetheart, Driver Harry Jeffs of the Royal Field Artillery who was in hospital in Cambridge Military Hospital in Aldershot. Harry, a farmer before the war, had received an injury to his left leg in 1913. The injury proved to be so severe that military service aggravated it. After Ruth left the hospital, she immediately wrote a postcard on her way home on the train back to Warrington. Her writing so shaky and poor that she must have written her message with the postcard perched on her lap on the jolting train.

Just a line dear Harry. I am writing this on the train. Hoping you will get better soon. I am thinking about you all the time. Please excuse writing. Cheer up dear. Best love and kisses, Ruth

Driver Harry Jeffs was discharged from the army on 2 August 1916 aged 23, having served eighteen months in France.

Gunner John William Wright Oxley of the Royal Field Artillery, who had joined the Territorial Army in 1910 aged seventeen, was wounded in Malta on 8 July 1916. He was sent to the 2nd Western Hospital in Manchester to recuperate, where he remained until November 1916. As some point, he was transferred to the Woodlands Hospital in Britain mentioned in his postcard.[6:11] Whilse at Woodlands, he took a shine to one of his nurses. When he returned to duty in Egypt in 1917, he wrote her this postcard. The EEF in his message was the Egyptian Expeditionary Force. John's use of the slang 'Eggwhipped' for Egypt is just one of the many examples of the slang used by British troops during the First World War. Gunner Oxley was injured once more in September 1918, after being poisoned by gas, and discharged from the army because of the effects of the gas in January 1919.

The postcard on the following page from Compton House Hospital in Sherborne, Dorset, the soldiers are wearing their 'hospital blues'. This was a uniform worn by an injured soldier who was not an officer, once he was in Britain, in place of his regular army uniform. A few British military hospitals in France also used the hospital blues uniform. The suit was made of flannel which was blue in colour, and worn with a white shirt and a red woven tie. The blue jacket was turned back to reveal deep white lapels. The uniform was worn with great pride as it represented a man's military service and the

Greetings and Heartfelt Wishes to Nurse

Somewhere in Eggwhipped. Dear Sister R, just a card to let you know am getting on alright. What do you think of this card? Only one thing wrong with it 'When days were long and dreary' They never were for me. I only wish I was back at Woodlands. Don't forget to save Hoskins and me a bed please. Remember me very kindly to all please. I trust all are enjoying the best of health. I don't like Eggwhipped Sister. My address 915023 A Battery 44th Brigade, R.F.A. EEF. Kindest regards Sincerely yours J.W.O. (Have left Egypt now.)

wounds he had suffered for King and Country. It also stopped the man being attacked by civilians, or being given a white feather (the symbol of cowardice), if he walked through the town of his hospital. The soldiers often wore their military (khaki) dress cap with its regimental cap badge. The uniform was compulsory for 'other ranks' whereas officers were allowed to keep their normal uniforms but wore an armband denoting that they had been wounded while in action.[6:12]

Compton House Hospital, Sherborne, Dorset

7 June 1918: Dear Queenie, just a postcard for you. This is a photo of the boys here with daddy. I hope your hand is better by this time. It is raining here today. Love to you and mummy and to all at home. From Daddy

Alf was a soldier with the Middlesex Regiment when he was photographed with his sweetheart on Hastings beach in July 1916. The day they spent on Hasting beach caught as a happy snapshot on a single day in time by local photographer A. M. Breach. Their only identification is the inscription on the back 'Alf & Pat, July 1916' and Alf's army cap badge.

The next postcard is undated and sent home by Lizzie's husband, Tom, who was in hospital somewhere in Britain. Tom had been sent some distance away from his home and was apart from his wife during Christmas and New Year, so he sent her this postcard. The ward had been decorated for Christmas with hanging paper chains and foliage draped from the ceiling with greenery on the central table. The shape and the layout of the room suggests that this was a purpose-built hut, rather than a room in a stately home.

Dearest Lizzie, just a card, hoping you will like it. It is the photo of our ward taken the day before Christmas Day. See if you can pick me out, you cannot see much of me. This is all I could afford, so do not sell this one or give it away as I can get no more. Well dearest, I wish you many happy days in the coming New Year. Goodbye dearest, let me know if you can pick me out. Love to you both. I am your loving husband, Tom

Another ward decorated for Christmas can be seen in this next postcard, where an unknown young soldier had placed a cross to mark himself (second from the right, second row).

This is where all the fun comes off. The best hospital in England. I have put a cross where I am.

"POOR MAN! AND HAVE YOU BEEN
WOUNDED AT THE FRONT?"

"NO, MA'AM————AT THE BACK!"

Gunner Alfred Ellis of the Royal Garrison Artillery was injured and in a hospital in Hazel Grove, Stockport in Manchester. His postcard to his mother was drawn by the well-known humourist postcard artist Donald McGill. Its subject of a soldier in hospital blues had obviously caught Alfred's eye and he sent it to his mother in Cleethorpes. As she lived over a hundred miles away from her son's hospital, his mother's visits to his bedside must have been long and arduous journeys for her. Hopefully his mother's sense of humour matched her son's taste in comic postcards.

Gunner A. C. Ellis, 175445, Royal Garrison Artillery, Stockport. June 2nd 1915. Dear Mother, just a line to say I received your parcel and also letter. I am being moved from here tomorrow, 3rd June. So do not come as you would miss me. Will write letter when I get to new address. Your loving son, Alf

Good Health!

GLAD TO SEE YOU'RE "GETTING ROUND" SO NICELY!

Pte Harold G. Frow of the West Yorkshire Regiment was in hospital in Bradley Gate Sanatorium in Huddersfield when he received this comic postcard of a wounded soldier in his hospital blues with a pretty nurse perched on his armchair.

Hope you are enjoying yourself this fine weather. Is this all you have to do in [the] army? Ann

Brighton Grammar School in Sussex was requisitioned in the initial weeks of the war and became the Second Eastern General Hospital. During the early part of the war, wounded soldiers in Britain were a novelty. The postcard below demonstrates that great crowds visited wounded soldiers, and these trips appeared to have been a good 'day out' for many. The photograph below was taken during the early weeks of the war; the soldiers were the survivors of the original British Expeditionary Force and wounded during the war's opening battles of August and September 1914. This was possibly the first time local people had seen wounded soldiers home from the war.

BRITISH WOUNDED HEROES AT GRAMMAR SCHOOL BRIGHTON · SEPT 1914 ·

Above: British Wounded Heroes at Grammar School Brighton, September 1914
Postmarked 2 October 1914: Dear Nellie, we went to see the soldiers yesterday & Nin & I went to Worthing last night to hear a concert party. Goodbye. Love from Rene

Right: Jack wrote to his sweetheart Nancy, a nurse in Whitchurch urging her to visit him.

My dear Nancy, just a few lines to let you know I am still in hospital longing to see you. Do come and see me Thursday if you can. I think it will be the last time we will be able to see one another for some time. Yours effect, Jack xxxxxxxxxxx

At Duty's Call

Though sad our hearts and loth to part
At Duty's stern decree,
Yet think how joyously we'll meet
When I come back to thee.

The navy had its own arrangements for its wounded and sick sailors, and these arrangements were slightly different to the army. The postcard below, a formal posed photograph with several men wearing their medals, is of a navy ambulance train, with its staff of Royal Navy Medical Assistants and nurses on their way to Leith in Scotland.

Below is a photograph of Surgeon Vice-Admiral Sir James Porter KCB, KCMG, LLD, MD, MA (1851–1935), along with Staff Surgeon Armin Gascoigne Vavasour Elder (1880–1940) of the Royal Naval Volunteer Reserve[6:13], with Nurse Sister Fry and Nurse Sister Thomas. Sir James had been the honorary surgeon to the King and medical director-general of the Royal Navy before his 1913 retirement. He came out of retirement during the First World War and was Principal Hospital Transport Officer for the Mediterranean during the Gallipoli Campaign of April 1915 to January 1916. It is unknown when this picture was taken but it is likely to have been sometime after the beginning of 1916 when both men had returned to Britain from Gallipoli.

Both trains in the postcard bear the name plaques of the L&NWR (London & North Western Railways) with the train on the left bearing the number of 9763 and on the right, 8767. The L&NWRconstructed a fleet of five navy ambulance trains for the Admiralty between September 1914 and March 1918.

Naval ambulance trains were significantly different from army ambulance trains. For the latter, patients were manually transferred into a cot within the train from an army stretcher. This cot was fixed to the side of the army ambulance train, therefore would have caused considerable discomfort and the possibility of further injury to the wounded soldier while he was transferred from stretcher to the train's cot. For a naval ambulance train, the injured man was placed into a cot on his ship, and then that same cot was attached to the side of the carriage of the naval ambulance train. Thus, the injured sailor was not moved at all once he had been placed on a cot on his ship; the same cot served as both bed and stretcher while he was transported to a hospital in Britain.[6:14]

Officers from left to right: Sister Thomas, Surgeon Elder, Sir James Porter & Sister Fry. The train is our hospital train which was half on each line, as soon as we were taken we started for Leith. The fellow in white is the chef.

Chapter 7
Armistice and Peace

LONDON'S GREAT VICTORY MARCH:
Naval Detachments passing Hyde Park Corner.

In 1918, on the eleventh hour of the eleventh day of the eleventh month, the fighting finally stopped; the First World War was at its end. The Allies and Germany signed the Armistice in a French railway carriage within the forest of Compiègne in Picardy. However, for many British men and women still on active duty, their war was far from over. The first of the various peace treaties which marked the end of the First World War, the Treaty of Versailles, was not signed between the Allies and Germany until the end of Paris Peace Conference in June 1919. Further treaties followed with the Allies' other former enemies: the Treaty of Saint-Germain-en-Laye was signed on 10 September 1919 (Austria), the Treaty of Neuilly-Sur-Seine on 27 November 1919 (Bulgaria), the Treaty of Trianon on 4 June 1920 (Hungary), and the Treaty of Sèvres on 10 August 1920 (Turkey).[7:1] Until these peace treaties between the Allies and their former enemies were agreed and signed, British troops remained overseas and were not demobbed nor discharged. This next selection of postcards and their messages all date from after the Armistice of 11 November 1918. They were sent to and from people within Britain, and sent home from British soldiers still 'On Active Duty'.

In the immediate aftermath of the Armistice, the relief felt at the end of a long and painful war was palpable throughout Britain. Large crowds assembled in central London to celebrate the end of the war and an unknown photographer caught some of those hordes of people streaming through Pall Mall.

Some of Our Victory Guns, London
> Sent from Auntie G in London to Wilfrid in Gloucester. 18 November 1918: I came along Pall Mall today and saw all these guns lined up along both sides of the road. I got this card there as I thought it would interest you. The guns are all sorts & sizes & are marked with the name of the regiments who captured them. Children climb all over them – just as they do the one in the park. Love from Auntie G

Peace with Honour
Sent from Blackpool to Barnsley in Yorkshire.
29 December 1918:

> Dear Arthur, hope you are having a good time
> and have found all well at home. I am having the
> happiest time of my life. So cheer up and best
> wishes for a Happy and Prosperous New Year.

The next postcard makes reference to the flu. The deadly influenza pandemic, which started in January 1918 and lasted until 1920, infected between 3 and 5 per cent of the world's population. No continent or country was immune from its devastation. Its impact and the deaths directly caused by the pandemic was just as deadly as the fighting had been during the First World War.[7:2]

Peace
Sent to Bishopstoke in Southampton:

> 1 December 1918: Dear Ethel, I saw
> these 'Peace' cards in town yesterday, and
> thought you would like one. And if you see
> any will you send me one, as I should like
> some for my collection. I hope you have
> all escaped the 'flu. We have escaped so
> far, though I have been in bed a week with
> liver and rheumatism again, and don't feel
> special yet. The 'flu is very bad around here
> yet. I heard from Fairfield 2 weeks ago,
> John Drew was expecting to be called up
> in the next 8 days (after October 28th) but
> don't suppose he will now. Isn't it a blessing
> 'tis over & we will be able to say 'peaceful
> Xmas' this year? Love to all, from Lil

The relief and joy felt at the end of the war was also evident overseas. During the early days of the First World War, King Albert of Belgium, had led his army against the German army. However, the German army almost totally overran the country and between August 1914 and November 1918 occupied 95 per cent of Belgium. Refugees flooded out of the country seeking sanctuary in countries such as Britain, France and the Netherlands, and the Belgium government went into exile. King Albert stayed in Belgium and continued to lead his army in the area of the River Yser; a tiny corner of unoccupied Belgium which the Belgium army had fiercely defended against the German army in October 1914. During the final Hundred Days Offensive, which started in August 1918 by the Allies, small parts of Belgium became liberated from the German occupation. However, the majority of the country was not liberated until the Armistice.

On Friday 22 November 1918, King Albert, with his wife and children and accompanied by Britain's Prince Albert (later King George VI), made their triumphant entrance into Brussels, Belgium's capital. Newspapers reported the procession was led by detachments of the American army, and also present were units from the British, French and Belgium armies. Crowds of Belgium people lined the streets to welcome their king home, who processed through the streets of his capital on a white horse.[7:3]

Dick, a British soldier stationed in Brussels, sent a postcard home to Britain of the jubilant Belgium procession. He sent it to mark Christmas 1918; the first Christmas of the peace.

entrée de la famille Royale et des troupes Alliées à Bruxelles le 22 Novembre 1918. — LUX Brux

22 November 1918
The entrance of the royal family and the Allied troops into Brussels. Brussels, Xmas 1918, Love from Dick

On Sunday 26 January 1919, King Albert reviewed brigades of the Third Division of the British army. During the review, the Belgian King and his son were mounted on horses outside the royal palace in Brussels. The British Prince of Wales (later King Edward VIII) and his brother, Prince Albert (later King George VI) were also present. There were so many British troops to be reviewed that the march-past took more than two hours, and a large crowd of Belgians assembled to watch the review. Newspapers reported that snow fell heavily throughout the march-past but it did not deter the jubilant crowds or troops.[7:4]

Above: Boulevard du Regent, Brussels, 27 January 1919

> Dear friends, this is one of the roads we marched on our triumphal march past the King of the Belgians on Sunday. Having a grand time until Tuesday morning in a very fine city not at all knocked about but everything is so awful. Yours etc. J. Day

Right: Sent from Charleroi to Chelsea, London, 26 November 1918

> Dear Doll, this is some place, the best we have ever struck in Belgium. Would like to stay here until we leave for home, and with luck, we shall do so. There is tons of work just now. Love L

Above and below are two postcards, which were sent in the early weeks after the Armistice from two unnamed British soldiers and were both posted from another Belgium location; Charleroi. The postcards are pre-war images; much of the area of Charleroi, a town which had strategic implications because of its location on the river Sambre, had been destroyed in the early days of the war. Fierce fighting took place between the French and German armies between 21 and 23 August 1914 during the Battle of Charleroi. The French were defeated and had to retreat after the battle and the

German army occupied the town. Immediately after the Armistice, part of the British Army marched through Belgium on its way to occupy Germany.

Avenue de Waterloo, Charleroi
Sent to Framlingham, Suffolk. 24 December 1918

> Dear mum & dad, just a postcard hope you are well. This is a postcard of a town I passed through on my journey up Belgium. I hope you got my letter alright. Hope to see you soon, love from your Dick

Post-war postcards arrived back in Britain from all over the world; including Germany who had once been Britain's enemy, but was now a conquered country. Under the terms of first the November 1918 Armistice and then the subsequent June 1919 Treaty of Versailles, the German city of Cologne (and other areas of the Rhineland) were occupied by the Allies after the end of the First World War. Regiments of the British Army marched into Germany in early December 1918. In December 1918, the advanced troops of the British Army crossed over the Rhine to commence their occupation of Cologne. Kenneth, a soldier who wrote home to Portsmouth, sent the following message on his picture postcard of Cologne's great cathedral.

> 11 December 1918: At Cologne at last – but we haven't had much chance of seeing it as the town is out of bounds. We are spending a few days here making ourselves look pretty for the march over the Rhine. Love and best wishes for Xmas and the New Year to all the family. Kenneth.

The next postcard, although sent in March 1919, shows the British mounted cavalry entering Cologne in December 1918.

British Calvary, Cologne, Germany
Postmarked 18 March 1919

Dear E, this is photo of the
British Calvary entering
Cologne. I hope you will like
these postcards. Cheerio Sid

14 January 1919: Dear Marion, received your very welcome letters the other day &
am pleased to hear you are all keeping well. You say you had a quiet New Year but
I don't think it could have been as bad as mine. Photo is of a place I was on guard at
for a few days, just coming up to Hogmanay night. Give my kindest regards to all and
accept [my] best wishes, from Jock

Jock of the Royal Field Artillery wrote from the town of Ohligs in the Stadt of Solingen,
Germany. He was on duty during late December 1918, guarding the Town Hall. His first
New Year's Eve of the Peace was a miserable time for him.
Various regiments of the British Army were also still in France after November 1918.
One homesick father returned from his leave home, and sent his daughter a postcard
showing the French town of Rouen with the following message.

Rouen, Tuesday 9am, 26 February 1919: My darling treasure, a week ago since I bade
you farewell quickly gone. Thank you for your letter, there's a reply in mama's written
last night for you. Has mamma seen Miss P. since I left? It is a beautiful day, frosty
morn. I am as well as usual, and I trust you each so. You will remember me telling you
of my crossing here regularly. Lots of Daddy's best love xx

When they were off-duty, some men and women took the opportunity to do limited
sight-seeing and also took in local walks. Hilda sent a postcard of the Luxembourg
Palace in Paris to her home in Birmingham, and described her visit to the French capital.
She was possibly a nurse at one of the military hospitals in Rouen. Despite the end of
the war, the hospitals were still busy with the endless new arrivals of injured and sick
men and female nurses, many of whom were suffering from the flu.

Rouen, 24 April 1919, Dear Gertie, went to gay Paris Good Friday, a guide from the
YMCA showed us around. I had a topping time. I've noticed your brother's signature
on several letters going through post.[i.e. as an army censor] When is he expecting to
get home? We heard today that we are going to be kept in France for a long time yet.
Hilda.

Sgt Alfred Peel wrote to his family in Manchester with a postcard (seen on the next
page) of the French seaside town of Trouville in Normandy photographed before the war.

28   TROUVILLE. — La Plage et les Villas. — LL.

France 15 February 1919: Dear mother and sister, thanks very much for letter 29, will answer tomorrow. Just had a walk as far as you can see on this photo. Just started to rain. Very busy here. Glad to hear that you are keeping well as I am in the pink. Pat Naps [dog] and stroke Kitty [cat] for me. Your loving brother

Corporal E. Clayton Gawdy sent the following message home to his family in Liverpool. From the censor's signature on his postcard, it is interesting to note that while postcards sent post-war from the Western Front still had to pass the eagle-eye of the censor and where signed by a censor, the towns and locations of the soldiers were no longer scored through.

LE TRÉPORT. — Panorama pris de la Falaise.-L

Sunday 17 August 1919: Having a weekend at Le Tréport. It is a nice change after Abbeville. The sea is A.1. and we had a fine bath this morning. We are sitting on the cliff this afternoon and there is a fine view.

Many people from all the services were anxious to be demobbed and return home to their families. Henry Gordon Boyack, a clerk in France with the Royal Air Force, had joined the service in March 1917 when it was still the Royal Flying Corp. In February

1919, he was located in the area around Le Tréport in Normandy. Two postcards to his sweet-heart Jean G. McIntosh of Dennistoun, Glasgow have survived.

> 6 February 1919: Was disappointed yesterday, there being no post for me. We had a heavy fall of snow and everything is white this morning. There is brilliant sun and the place looks rather pretty. Will write you today. Glad to say I am feeling much better now. Hoping this will find you keeping well. Regards to all and warmest love. Harry
> 12 February 1919: Many thanks for your welcome letter received last night. Glad to know you are well. The frost is still as hard as ever. Some of our boys were passed for demobilisation yesterday. Now that they have started I hope that they will get on quickly. Glad to hear Ralph has got home. I suppose that he has checked for the A.O.O. I thought he would have got home for good. Will write tonight. Warmest love Harry

Harry had to wait a further three months before he was demobbed; his service records show that he finally left France on 9 May 1919. After he returned home from France, Harry married his sweetheart, Jean McIntosh, in 1919.

The sender of the following postcard, which is dated as late as 30 December 1919, more than a year after the Armistice, expressed his displeasure that he was still in France by using an abundance of exclamation marks to litter his short message.

> France 30 December 1919: Many thanks for card & Xmas wishes! You will observe I'm still here! God knows when I am leaving! 'Sooner the better'. Excuse this unpleasant reminder of France in the shape of a postcard!!! Will write tomorrow. Kindest regards

During the course of 1919, soldiers were demobilised and sent back to Britain. After the signing of the Treaty of Versailles in June 1919, large street parties and community celebrations were held throughout the towns and villages of Britain to celebrate. The British Prime Minster persuaded the architect Edwin Lutyen to build a temporary Cenotaph (or 'empty tomb') in Whitehall for the nation's July Peace Celebrations. Originally constructed of plaster and wood, the Cenotaph was unveiled on 19 July 1919 and was meant to remain only a few months. However, it proved so popular with the politicians and mourning British public that the Cenotaph was made permanent and rebuilt using Portland Stone.[7:5] The permanent Cenotaph was unveiled at 11 a.m. on the 11 November 1920; two years after the Armistice was signed in a French railway carriage within the forest of Compiègne in Picardy. On the same day, the unknown warrior was brought back from the Western Front and transported with great solemnity by gun carriage through the hushed crowd-lined streets of London, past the King and his Generals at the Cenotaph, to be laid to rest within the hallowed walls of the ancient Westminster Abbey.[7:6]

> The Great Silence London. Cenotaph unveiling and unknown warrior's internment: The two minutes' silence most impressively observed throughout the Metropolis on Thursday morning. On the first stroke of eleven o'clock all traffic and business ceased, and pedestrians stood bareheaded, and paid their silent tribute to the dead. The unveiling the Cenotaph and the interment of the unknown British warrior in Westminster Abbey were attended with impressiveness never before witnessed. Thousands lined the route of the procession. A Field Marshal's salute of nineteen guns was the signal that the

cortege, surrounded by all the panoply of war, had started from Victoria Station, headed firing party and the massed bands of the Guards. The King and the Prince of Wales, with the officers State, awaited the arrival of the body at the Cenotaph, which His Majesty unveiled, and the procession afterwards completed the journey to the Abbey. At the Abbey the body of the Unknown was laid rest in the presence of the King, the Queen, members the Royal Family, the Prime Minister and members the Government, delegations from the Houses of Parliament, representatives the Forces, and relatives of those who fell in the war. All telephonic and telegraphic communication in the country was suspended during the great silence. Services were held in many towns. At all the naval ports and military stations, in conformity with the King's message. Colours were lowered half-mast, all work ceased, and two minutes' silence was observed the Government servants and troops. The Union Jack was flown from half-mast at a good many business premises.

Western Gazette, Friday 12 November 1920

The unveiling of the permanent Cenotaph and the funeral procession of the Unknown Warrior, 11 November 1920.

The Tomb of the Unknown Warrior, Westminster Abbey, November 1920.

Notes

General

Wherever possible, the senders and recipients of the postcards within this book have been researched using census returns, civil records, military records, war diaries, service records and national/local newspapers. To this end, the online subscription services, FindMyPast, Forces War Records and The British Newspaper Archive have proved invaluable. Also, the Commonwealth War Graves Commission's War Dead online database and The National Archive's British Army Medal Index Cards have been extensively consulted.

Introduction

1 British Postal Museum & Archive, *The Post Office and the First World War*, http://www.postalheritage.org.uk/explore/history/firstworldwar/.
2 Pratt, E., *British Railways and the Great War, Volume II*, (London: Selwyn and Blount Limited, 1921), p. 1090. This is a gem of a book and compulsive reading for the logistics of the First World War within Britain. However, Pratt's yearly totals for the transport of mail do not tally up with the British Postal Museum's totals. It is difficult to determine which figures are correct. I have gone with Pratt, as his account was written only a few years after the end of the war.

1 Keep the Home Fires Burning

1:1 Barker, C., *The Long, Long Trail: The British regular army of 1914–1918*, (1996-2016), http://www.1914-1918.net/regular.htm.
1:2 Barker, C., *The Long, Long Trail: Kitchener's Army*, (1996–2016), http://www.1914-1918.net/kitcheners.htm.
1:3 Keitch, C., *Imperial War Museums: Recruitment and Conscription*, (2016), http://www.iwm.org.uk/learning/resources/recruitment-and-conscription.
1:4 *Litchfield Mercury*, Prince's First Day as a soldier, Friday 14 August 1914.
1:5 *Coventry Evening Telegraph*, Civil Marksmen to train recruits, 17 August 1914.
1:6 James, N. D. G., *Gunners at Larkhill a History of the Royal School of Artillery*, (Gresham Books, 1983).
1:7 Allen, T., *Bruce Bairnsfather WW1 Postcards*, (2014), http://www.worldwar1postcards.com/bruce-bainsfather.php.

1:8 Royal Air Force, *39 Squadron*, (2016), http://www.raf.mod.uk/organisation/39squadron.cfm.
1:9 Morris, J. *The German Air Raids on Great Britain 1914-1918*, (1925).

2 Greetings from the Trenches

2:1 Royal Mail Group, *Charting the First World War – 1914*, (2016), http://www.royalmailgroup.com/about-us/heritage/charting-first-world-war-1914.
2:2 The Oxonian was built in 1898 and, by the time of the First World War, was used by the Leyland Line of Liverpool. It was hired on several occasions as a troop ship transporting British soldiers to and from the Western Front. For further information, consult: The Ships List, *Leyland Line Fleet,* (1997–2016), http://www.theshipslist.com/ships/lines/leyland.shtml.
2:3 National Army Museum, *Field Marshal Fredrick Sleigh Roberts*, 1st Earl Roberts, (2016), http://www.nam.ac.uk/exhibitions/online-exhibitions/britains-greatest-general/frederick-roberts.
2:4 Baker, C., *The Long, Long Trail: Life in the Trenches of the First World War*, (1996-2016), http://www.longlongtrail.co.uk/soldiers/a-soldiers-life-1914-1918/life-in-the-trenches-of-the-first-world-war/.
2:5 The volunteer organisation, the Young Man's Christian Association (YMCA), was crucial to the First World War effort. Early on in the war, it established recreational and refreshment centres all over Britain and in 1915 received permission to open similar centres in France. For further information, consult: Baker, C., *The Long, Long Trail: YMCA and other volunteer organisations*, (1996–2016), http://www.1914-1918.net/ymca.htm.
2:6 The University of Oxford have published a zoom-able map of the wartime town of Étaples showing the location of its numerous military hospitals, camps and army post offices. University of Oxford, *The First World War Poetry Digital Archive: Map of Étaples Training Camp*, http://ww1lit.nsms.ox.ac.uk/ww1lit/gwa/document/9127/4558.
2:7 Étaples Military Camp was the site of an infamous mutiny by British Army soldiers in September 1917.
2:8 There was no known truce between the British and the Germans during Christmas 1916. Two years earlier, at Christmas 1914, British and German soldiers had fraternized with each other in no-man's land. For further information regarding the famous 1914 Christmas Truce, consult: Cole, K. *Christmas Truce 1914,* (2014), http://worldwidegenealogy.blogspot.co.uk/2014/12/christmas-truce-1914.html.
2:9 The Lusitania Resource, History, *Passengers & Crew Biographies, and Lusitania Facts, (2003-2016)*, http://www.rmslusitania.info/.
2:10 The raids took place on the night of 19/20 October 1917 by thirteen zeppelins. The Midlands, Eastern Counties and London all became victims of the raids with a total of thirty-six people killed and a further fifty-five people injured. For further information, consult: Morris, J. *The German Air Raids on Great Britain 1914-1918*, (1925).
2:11 The zeppelin attacks Fred referred to took place on the nights of 31 July/1 August and 2/3 August. The Germans dropped 100 bombs over Kent, Norfolk, Suffolk, Cambridgeshire, Isle of Ely and Lincolnshire during the former raid. During the latter raid, 137 bombs were dropped over Norfolk, East Suffolk and Kent. Miraculously, no one was killed or injured..

2:12 For a photograph of Charles Frederick Barnes driving a pre-war char-a-banc, The Swiftsure, between Clacton to St Oysth, consult: Baker, T.A., *Clacton-on-Sea in Old Picture Postcards*, (1984), p.49.

2:13 My grateful thanks to members of the Facebook page *Clacton and District Local History Centre* who provided information about Barnes Coaches of Clacton.

2:14 Scally, H., History Extra: *10 ways Christmas was celebrated during the First World War*, (2014), http://www.historyextra.com/feature/first-world-war/10-ways-christmas-was-celebrated-during-first-world-war.

3 The Nurses' Story

I am grateful to the following people who helped with the story of VAD Clara Emily Mary Woolnough. Sue Light from Scarlet Finders for her extensive help and knowledge generously shared regarding the nursing services of the First World War. Louise Mann of Levington and Stratton Hall Village Archive, who provided extensive details regarding the Woolnough family of Levington, Suffolk. Clara's great-nephew, Barrie Everson, who is the grandson of Clara's brother George, and his children Joanne and Simon. The Everson family have been extremely generous in their support of my recounting the story of their aunt, and kindly provided more family ephemera, and also shared family recollections.

3:1 British Red Cross, *War-time volunteers and personnel records*, http://www.redcross.org.uk/About-us/Who-we-are/Museum-and-archives/resources-for-researchers/Volunteers-and-personnel-records and Light, S, *Voluntary Aid Detachments (VADs)*. http://www.scarletfinders.co.uk/181.html.

3:2 Clara Emily Mary Woolnough's and Gertrude Emma Unwin's VAD service history in this chapter are all from the British Red Cross' online database *First World War volunteers* available at http://www.redcross.org.uk/About-us/Who-we-are/History-and-origin/First-World-War.

3:3 Neufchatel Hardelot Office of Tourism, *A little history*, (2016), http://www.hardelot-tourisme.com/presentation-station-neufchatel-hardelot-plage-eng.html.

3:4 McCarthy M., the Matron-in-Chief, The National Archives: *War Diary of Matron in Chief, British Expeditionary Force, France and Flanders*, WO95/3988-91[transcribed by Sue Light, http://www.scarletfinders.co.uk/110.html].

3:5 All statistics, reports and information regarding Number 25 General Hospital within this chapter have been taken from the hospital's War Diaries: The National Archives, *Lines of Communication Troops: War Diary of 25 General Hospital*, WO95/4085.

3:6 Kellett, A.M, *Through these lines: No. 25 General Hospital*, http://throughtheselines.com.au/research/hardelot-plage.

3:7 For an extensive summary and day-by-day account of the Battles of the Somme, consult: Baker, C, *The Long, Long Trail: The Battles of the Somme 1916*, (1996-2016) http://www.1914-1918.net/bat15C.htm.

3:8 Gunner Richard Henry Cripps, aged 22 and son of Richard and Edith Cripps of Woolwich, was killed in action 25 September 1916 and buried at Bruay Communal Cemetery Extension.

3:9 Second Supplement to the *London Gazette* (24 May 1918), https://www.thegazette.co.uk/London/issue/30704/supplement/6174, p.6175.

3:10 Doyle, P., Doomed Youth: The war dead of Woolwich Polytechnic, 1914–1918 (2009).

4 To My Dear Children

4:1 Many postcards sent home by fathers to their children were French embroidered silk postcards. The most authoritative book regarding this type of postcard is: Collins, I., *An Illustrated History of the Embroidered Silk Postcard* (Gabrian Antiques, 2001). The author of *Embroidered Silk Postcards* has expanded his research since his book's publication in 2001. His updated research can be consulted at: Collins, I., *Embroidered Silk Postcards*, https://sites.google.com/site/embroideredsilkpostcards/home.

5 The War on the Land and in the Air

5:1 Preston Grammar School Association, *The Great War 1914–1918: War Memorial and Records*, (2008), http://www.ww1.pgsassociation.org.uk/.

5:2 Charles' war service records: The National Archives, *Air Ministry: Department of the Master-General of Personnel: Officers' Service Records – Charles Edward Pullen*, AIR 76/414/76. Reginald's war service records: The National Archives, *British Army Soldiers and officers in the First World War*, WO 363.

5:3 Commonwealth Graves Commission, *Vermelles British Cemetery*, (2016), http://www.cwgc.org/find-a-cemetery/cemetery/2000089/vermelles%20british%20cemetery.

5:4 Barker, C., *The Long, Long Trail: The Battle of Neuve Chapelle*, (1996-2016), http://www.1914-1918.net/bat9.htm.

5:5 The National Archives, War Dairy: 1/7th Battalion, King's Liverpool Regiment: January 1916 – April 1919, WO 95/2927/1.

5:6 Commonwealth War Graves Commission, *Battle of Albert: 1–3 July 1916*, (2016), http://www.cwgc.org.

5:7 The National Archives War Dairy: *1/7th Battalion, King's Liverpool Regiment*, WO95/29271.

5:8 Details regarding the battalion's actions during the Battle of Pilckem Ridge, part of the Third Battle of Ypres, are from the battalion's War Diary. The National Archives, War Dairy: *1/5th Battalion, South Lancashire Regiment: January 1916 – July 1919*, WO 95/2929/2.

5:9 Edmonds, J. E. (ed.), *Military Operations France and Belgium 1917: Messines and Third Ypres (Passchendaele)*, (Imperial War Museum: 1992).

5:10 Supplement to the *Edinburgh Gazette* (27 September 1917), https://www.thegazette.co.uk/Edinburgh/issue/13146/page/2058, p.2058.

5:11 Supplement to the *London Gazette* (9 January 1918), https://www.thegazette.co.uk/London/issue/30466/supplement/637, p.637.

5:12 My grateful thanks to Mark Sheppard for his extensive research on the 9th Battalion of the East Lancashire Regiment and his discovery that Reg had been posted to this battalion after the Armistice.

5:13 The post-war movements of the 9th Battalion are from the battalion's war diary. The National Archives, *War Diaries of the 9th Battalion East Lancashire Regiment, November 1915 to February 1919*, WO 95/4851.

5:14 The Virtual Aviation Museum, *De Havilland DH9A*, (2006–2016), http://www.militaryfactory.com/.

5:15 The National Archives, *Air combat reports: 49 Squadron, Royal Air Force* (June 1918), AIR 1/1223/204/5/2634/89.

5:16 The National Archives, *Reports on aeroplane and personnel causalities*, (11 June 1918-20 June 1918), AIR 1/856/204/5/410 [Compiled by 49 Squadron Association]

5:17 49 Squadron Association, *Beauvois Airfield*, (2016), http://www.49squadron.co.uk/airfields/af1_beauvois2.

5:18 49 Squadron Association, *World War 1 Losses*, (2016), http://www.49squadron.co.uk/losses/ww1_losses.

5:19 The National Archives, *Air combat reports: 49 Squadron* (August 1918), AIR/1/1223/204/5/2634.

6 Hospital Blues

6:1 For a comprehensive list of military and auxiliary hospitals located in Britain, consult: Baker, C., *The Long, Long Trail: The Military Hospitals at Home*, (1996–2016) http://www.1914-1918.net/hospitals_uk.htm and British Red Cross, *List of Auxiliary Hospitals in the UK During the First World War*, www.redcross.org.uk/WW1. For a comprehensive list of hospitals on the Western Front, consult: Baker, C., *The Long, Long Trail: The Base Hospitals in France*, (1996–2016), http://www.1914-1918.net/hospitals.htm.

6:2 For an account on the military hospitals established in Étaples, including the St John's Ambulance Brigade's hospital: Meynell, E. W (MD), *Some Account of the British Military Hospitals of World War I at Etaples, in the orbit of Sir Almroth Wright*, Journal of the Royal Army Medical Corps, 1996 (p.43–47).

6:3 The Museum of the Order of St John, *Étaples Reports Project Introduction*, (2015), https://stjohnsgate.wordpress.com/category/etaples-reports-project-introduction/.

6:4 McCarthy M., the Matron-in-Chief, *The National Archives: War Diary of Matron in Chief, British Expeditionary Force, France and Flanders*, WO95/3990 [transcribed by Sue Light, http://www.scarletfinders.co.uk/91.html].

6:5 The bombing raids were widely reported in all British newspapers, and questions were asked in the House of Commons. For further information, consult: Commons and Lords Hansard, *The Official Report of debates in Parliament*, (31 July 1918) Vol 109 p.407–8.

6:6 The location of the St John's Ambulance Hospital is visible on the wartime map of Étaples military camp. Consult the map of Étaples at: University of Oxford, The First World War Poetry Digital Archive: *Map of Étaples Training Camp*, http://ww1lit.nsms.ox.ac.uk/ww1lit/gwa/document/9127/4558.

6:7 HMHS Asturias, (2016), https://en.wikipedia.org/wiki/HMHS_Asturias; and *Roll of Honour, Ships: HMHS Asturias* (2002–2016), http://www.roll-of-honour.com/Ships/HMHSAsturias.html.

6:8 British Red Cross, *General Overview of Joint War Committee Activities During the First World War*, www.redcross.org.uk/WW1, and British Red Cross, *Auxiliary Hospitals During the First World War*, www.redcross.org.uk/WW1.

6:9 Leeds Library, *The Gledhow Hall scrapbook*, (2014), http://secretlibraryleeds.net/2014/07/25/the-gledhow-hall-scrapbook/.

6:10 Westerham Town Partnership, *Life in Westerham in 1914*, (2012–2015), http://www.visitwesterham.org.uk/heritage/fww/1914-2.

6:11 There were three hospitals in Wigan known as Woodlands and a Woodlands Auxiliary Hospital in Kilcreggan in Scotland. It has been impossible to discover which one John recovered in.

6:12 Reznick, J. S., *The 'Convalescent Blues' in Frederick Cayley Robinson's 'Acts of Mercy'*, (2010), http://blog.wellcomelibrary.org/2010/06/the-convalescent-blues-in-frederick-cayley-robinsons-acts-of-mercy/.

6:13 Armin Gascoigne Vavasour Elder of the Royal Naval Volunteer Reserve (RNVR) was awarded the Distinguished Service Cross in April 1918. His citation appeared in the *London Gazette* of 16 April 1918 (issue number 30635, page 4646). 'In Recognition of his services in connection with Naval ambulance trains and sea hospital transport throughout the war. Actg. Staff Surgeon Elder was frequently under fire at the Gallipoli beaches.' He continued to serve in the Merchant Navy after the end of the First World War and died of illness while at sea on-board the HMS *Laurentic* on 13 June 1940, just months before the ship was torpedoed by a German Submarine in November 1940 during the Second World War.

6:14 Pratt, Edwin A., *British Railways and the Great War*, (London, 1921); p.567-568.

7 Armistice and Peace

7:1 MacMillian, M., *Peacemakers: Six Months that Changed the World*, (London: John Murray, 2001).

7:2 Billings, M., *The Influenza Pandemic of 1918*, (1997, revised 2005), https://virus.stanford.edu/uda/ and Kahn, K., *The 'Spanish' Influenza pandemic and its relation to World War I*, http://ww1centenary.oucs.ox.ac.uk/body-and-mind/the-spanish-influenza-pandemic-and-its-relation-to-the-first-world-war/.

7:3 *Daily Record Newspaper*, Belgium's Rich Reward: Press Association War Special, (25 November 1918).

7:4 *Lancashire Evening Post*, King Albert Reviews British Troops, (27 January 1919).

7:5 A&E Television Network, *This day in history: 19 July 1919 Cenotaph is unveiled in London*, http://www.history.com/this-day-in-history/cenotaph-is-unveiled-in-london.

7:6 Westminster Abbey, *Unknown Warrior*, (2016) http://www.westminster-abbey.org/our-history/people/unknown-warrior.

Appendix I

Post & Censor Marks of the Western Front

In addition to a postcard's message and addressee details, postcards from the First World War often hold a great deal of official information. Some of this information can be used for research purposes to track down the location of a division or brigade or unit of the postcard's sender. Nearly every postcard posted from the Western Front will contain at least three researchable official elements (although, of course, there are always exceptions to this rule). If a postcard does not contain any of these three elements but has the general appearance that it was sent from overseas, then it is likely it was posted inside an envelope. In these cases, the envelope would have received the usual official signature and/or censor/postmarks. This is particularly true for French embroidered silk postcards which were often sent back to Britain in their protective envelopes. If a postcard has only one or two of these official elements (but not all three) it could be that human error caused the missing elements to be omitted. Or that the mark is so faint that it is hard to locate.

The official elements of mail from the Western Front are: 1) The handwritten countersignature of the censor; 2) a numbered censor mark stamped in ink; and 3) a dated and coded postmark (hand or machine) stamped in ink.

Official Element 1: Countersignature of the Censor

Every piece of mail from the Western Front was individually read and censored by junior officers. The censor's job was to read each postcard or letter and strikeout or totally obliterate with a blue pencil (or other means such as scratching out with a sharp implement) any identifiable details or information which would be disastrous if the mail fell into enemy hands. The censor scrutinised and censored both sides of postcards, including any printed captions, such as the local town's name. Once the censor had read the item and censored it, he countersigned the postcard (or envelope). After he countersigned it, he then stamped the postcard/envelope with a censor mark hand stamp. The censored mail then entered into the army's postal system for postmarking, sorting and onwards transmission.

Some censor signatures are firm readable signatures, others merely a squiggle. If it is difficult to identify the sender of a postcard but the postcard has a good clear censor signature (hopefully with an unusual surname), then sometimes it pays to research the man who censored the postcard. Censors also censored their own outgoing mail, so sometimes the censor's signature matches the sender's name, signature and/or handwriting.

Mail from the Western Front continued to be censored after the Armistice of 11 November 1914. With the various peace treaties not signed until 1919 and 1920, the authorities were clearly not taking any chances.

Above left: A particularly unhelpful censor's countersignature. Green? Queen? Gunner?

Above right: Clear countersignature but with the common surname of Robinson, so possibly not useful.

Above left: The surname of the sender of this postcard is not totally legible. However, the censor's countersignature in the top left corner is sufficiently clear and with an unusual name. His signature can be used to identify him via The National Archives' online First World War Medal Index Cards. This censor was George Francis Lambert-Porter of the West Yorkshire Regiment, later killed in action in June 1917 and recommended for a posthumous Victoria Cross. Once the name of this postcard's censor was established, there is only one name in the Medal Index archive which fits its sender; John J. Whitley, number 15/1755 of the West Yorkshire Regiment. Lambert-Porter's death places him (and therefore possibly also John J. Whitley) at Messines Ridge near Ypres on 8 June 1917. Sometimes researching the military career of a censor can provide extra context and detail for the sender of a postcard.

Above right: Postcard dated April 1918 from the Pullen brothers' collection (Chapter 5). The censor's signature is that of Charles himself; C. E. Pullen (bottom right edge of postcard). This is a clear signature leaving no doubt that the writer of the message also censored his own card; there are no other 'squiggles' on the postcard which could be the censor's signature. His countersignature is in the same ink and handwriting as the message; evidence that this was censored by Charles at the time he wrote his postcard. If this was a stand-alone postcard with no other details to give it context, the censor countersigning his own postcard would indicate that this postcard was probably from a junior officer. Charles was a (probationary) second lieutenant in April 1918, so was a junior officer and therefore permitted to censor his own message.

Official Element 2: Numbered Stamped Censor Mark

A numbered censor mark was stamped onto each postcard or envelope, normally with red ink, although other colours were used such as purple or black. The shape of the censor mark varied throughout the war and its shape given a type name. As each shape was used within a specific range of dates on the Western Front, the censor mark can give an approximate date for an individual postcard. This is particularly helpful if the separate dated postmark is unclear or partially missing. Many thousands of censor mark stamps were issued. Unfortunately, no official records exist listing each number on a censor stamp and to whom or to where it was issued. Moreover, the censor hand stamps were often exchanged between units every few months for extra security. However, the shape of the censor mark gives a good indication as to when the postcard was sent and possibly identifies its theatre of war.

Table 1: British Censor Marks Used on the Western Front

Date Used on the Western Front	Type	Shape of Mark	Examples
Until November 1914	CM1	Round	
December 1914 to March 1915	CM2	Square	
April 1915 to December 1915	CM3	Triangle	
January 1916 to October 1916	CM4	Hexagon	
November 1916 to September 1917	CM5	Oval	
October 1917 to post-war*	CM6	Rectangle	

*From 1918, some American divisions were also issued this type of censor mark from the British authorities.

Table 2: British Censor marks for Other Theatres of War

Other Theatres of War	Type	Shape of Mark	Examples
All Mediterranean theatres of war (including Egypt)*.	CM1, CM2, CM3, CM6	Circle, square, triangle, rectangle	As per Western Front examples.
Egypt and Salonika (includes Greece/Serbia/Albania etc.) from October 1917**.	CM7	Octagon	
Italy from April 1918***	CM8	Shield	

*From the start of the war until the dates in the rest of this table. However, these types were used at different times to the Western Front. For example, the author has in her collection postcards from Egypt with type CM2 (square) from December 1915 i.e. several months after it was no longer in use on the Western Front.

**Exclusive to these theatres of war.

***Exclusive to Italy.

Official Element 3: Dated and Numbered Stamped Postmark

Every piece of mail from the Western Front was date-stamped with a postmark made by a handstamp or machine stamp. Like a modern-day postmark, each part of the postmark can be used to identify details about when and where a piece of mail had been posted. Below are guidelines to the postmarks. However, as always, there will be exceptions to these parameters, so these are general rules.

- **Army/Field Post office:** This is the text at the top or start of the postmark. Field Post Offices were generally small mobile units attached to a brigade or division which moved with the army (although, as always, there are exceptions to this). An Army Post Office was normally a stationary unit so were mainly located at army bases (such as Étaples which had several Army Post Offices) or headquarters, or in major towns, or places which had good infrastructure such as St Omer or Rouen.
- **Shape of postmark:** A single ring encasing the postmark was normally used during 1914 – this is often known as a 'skeleton' postmark. From early 1915, this moved to a double ring. Both the single and double ring postmark indicate that a postcard was stamped by hand. From the middle of the war, machines were introduced into the main army post offices at Boulogne, Calais, Le Havre and Rouen. These machine-stamped postmarks are not encased in a circular mark but have wavy lines left and right of the words 'ARMY P.O. 1'. The number at the end indicated which main army post office had machine-stamped the mail: ARMY P.O. 1 for Le Havre, ARMY P.O. 2 for Rouen, ARMY P.O. 3 for Boulogne and ARMY P.O. 4 for Calais. As the machine-stamped postmarks was not a manual process, sometimes the wavy-lined postmark was

accidently stamped onto the postcard's front. The machine-made postmarks are quite long with the consequence that many machine-stamped postcards have only partial fragments of a postmark. There are some anomalies to machine-produced postmarks; for example the author has a postcard in her collection with a wavy-lined machine-made postmark for A.P.O. S.12 dated 13 January 1917, another Army Post Office which was also located in Le Havre.

- **Date:** The date can be in a couple of formats: DD MM YY (e.g. '11 MR 15' for 11 March 1915), MM DD YY (e.g. 'JU 30 15' for 30 June 1915).
- **Code:** At the bottom of the postmark is normally a code. This code will be all letters, all numbers, or letters followed by numbers. Each code represented a particular post office. Tracing details of this code could provide a substantial clue as to the whereabouts of the sender of a postcard at the date of its postmark. Peter Doyle, in his book *British Postcards of the First World War*, estimated that there are at least 1,600 different First World War postmarks. These codes were regularly swapped around; particularly from June 1916 onwards, after the British captured a train full of German mail which enabled the Allies to discover full details of the German army's positions. Therefore, identifying the location of a post office by its code number at the start of the war does not necessarily mean that numbered stamp will be with the same post office by the end of the war.

Table 3: Examples of Army and Field Post Office Postmarks

	Single circular Army Post Office postmark from December 1914. On this postmark, the year is only just visible. The number 13 at the bottom is the code for that particular Army Post Office.
	Double circular Army Post Office S.13 postmark from the postcard sent by Private Eric Perrin of the Honourable Artillery Company who, at this time, was patient in a military hospital in the town of Le Tréport, Picardy. His location indicates that S.13 was a stationary Army Post Office in Le Tréport.
	Army Post Office S.11 was located in Étaples, one of several army post offices in the town which contained many British and Canadian hospitals and a large military camp.
	Tell-tale wavy lines of the machine-stamped postmark. With the Army P.O. mark bearing the number 2, this postcard was sent from the main post office in Rouen.

 Only the hint of the machine-stamped Army Post Office postmark is visible on this card from VAD Clara Woolnough. The barely visible 'P.O.3' top right means that her card was posted at Boulogne Army Post Office. Underneath is the almost lost date-stamp 'N 16'. This could either be the month followed by year (e.g. June 1916), or the month followed by the day (e.g. June 16). However, the hexagonal type CM4 censor mark, together with Clara's own message, proves that this was posted 14 June 1916, shortly before the opening days of the Battles of the Somme.

Researching First World War Censor marks and Postmarks

The topic of First World War postal history with its associated postmarks and censor marks is vast. A complete list of all numbered censor marks and postmarks is far beyond the scope of this book. It requires its own specialist book written by an expert on the subject. Moreover, this is a fast changing field of specialisation with the majority of information painstakingly collated over numerous years (often entire lifetimes) by serious expert collectors or postal history societies. Therefore, the bibliography towards the end of this book includes books about the Western Front's postal history. Unfortunately, many of the books within this bibliography were privately published so had very small print runs. This has made these books incredibly difficult (and expensive) to obtain, even via the British inter-library loan scheme. If you have access to any of the six legal deposit libraries in the United Kingdom and Ireland, then you will be able to locate the books in one of those libraries.

Because the expert books are so difficult to locate, the starting point for researching a postcard and its censor/postmarks will probably be the internet. A good search engine with well-constructed search strings might be successful in locating a particular censor mark or postmark. There are also postal history experts selling First World War postcards on eBay and other internet auction sites. Again, it could be fruitful to enter a particular censor mark/postmark into an auction site's search engine to see what the results produce.

The online Great War Forum (http://1914-1918.invisionzone.com/forums/index.php) have some extremely knowledgeable and helpful members. It could be productive to join the forum and post a specific message with an image of the censor mark/postmark to receive help from members. Some forum members who have keen interest in First World War postal history will have access to the elusive postal history books with lists of censor marks and postmarks. If you do post on the forum, remember some basic etiquette: be polite, always thank the person who has helped you and, if you can, return the favour by helping someone else with their research.

Using the internet to research First World War postcards (or indeed, any internet research) comes with a caveat: do not believe everything you read on the internet. If, for example, you find on a website that your postmark came from the Somme area of France, make a note of this and the website where you found the information. However, only believe this information to be true if you can verify it with other research. For example, if the regimental diaries for your postcards date shows your soldier was nowhere near the Somme but in, say, Italy, then it is highly likely that the information you read about your postmark is wrong. Always check, double-check and triple-check any information gleaned from the internet.

Appendix II

Postcards as Primary Sources

Over the passage of the last 100 years, many people's first-hand accounts of the First World War in the form of their letters and/or their diaries have been lost or destroyed. However, one type of first-hand account which have survived in their tens of thousands are the postcards sent home during the conflict. The existence of this book is proof as to the huge number of postcards which have survived. If you have access to postcards sent to/from your own ancestors during 1914 to 1919, then analysing them as a primary source could reap rich rewards in terms of understanding your ancestor's war.

For any historian researching any form of primary source, a good starting point is to apply The 6 Ws of Primary Source Analysis. These principles apply to all primary sources with the aim to squeeze as much information as possible out of them. The general principle of the 6Ws is to apply six one-word prompts (or questions) to the postcard. What? When? Who? Where? Why? How? (The last one obviously is not a W but, as always, there are exceptions to rules!)

What: What are you looking at? This prompt is about whether the source is a public or private document. A public document would be, for example, the war diaries of a battalion; a document which could come under close scrutiny by someone other than its author such as an official or even generals and military leaders. A private document would normally be, for example, a personal letter; a document which would not be read by anyone else other than the intended recipient. A postcard could fall into the category of a private document. However, messages on First World War postcards (and also private letters posted from theatres of war) have to be classified as being semi-private. Although some letters from soldiers did get published in newspapers during the conflict, in general, the writer of a postcard/letter did not intend their writings to be published and were only to be read by their loved ones. However, the army censor, the army postman and even the local village postmaster/postmistress would all be able to read the entire contents of a postcard. Therefore, postcards written from a theatre of war during the conflict were written under restrictive conditions. The writer knew full well that his/her postcard would be censored, and that many people, including people from his/her own village, could and would read the message.

When: When was the postcard written and what was its timeline in context of the war? If the writer did not date it, can it be dated by researching the censor mark and/or the postmark (see Appendix 1). If it can be dated, can the postcard be put into its historical context of a specific battle or offensive? One of Reginald Pullen's postcards (Chapter 5) demonstrate that it was sent from the town of Albert just days after the

Battle of Albert in July 1916. The background knowledge about the Battle makes Reg's message regarding the town more interesting.

Who: Who wrote your postcard? A seemingly simple question but this one can be one of the hardest to answer. Use everything on the postcard to discover 'who' wrote your postcard.

Where: In the terms of a First World War postcard, the answer to this question might have to be assumed. It may have been sent from 'Somewhere in France' but exactly where was the writer situated when s/he wrote the message? A comfortable officers' mess at HQ, in a semi-comfortable billet in a French farmhouse, or in a reserve trench awaiting to move forward into the Front Line? Sometimes the handwriting can indicate where a person was when the postcard was written. Eloquent handwriting written in ink could indicate a comfortable location. A quickly dashed-off message full of mistakes and written in blue pencil could indicate pre or post battle conditions. Of course, in many cases 'where' a postcard was written can only be mere conjecture. However, imagining this can totally change its meaning. Many of the messages in Chapter 2 could only have been written in pre or post battle conditions or while the soldiers were resting in their billets/camps/tents.

Why: Why was the postcard with its message sent? In the context of a First World War postcard, this is normally an obvious answer; to reassure loved ones. Many tens of thousands of postcards exist with simple messages such as 'I hope this finds you as well as it finds me'. 'I am A1'. A hastily written postcard was often the only means a soldier had to connect with their families. Even the simplest 'Love to all at home' message is evocative that these were men (and women) far from home. Obviously, longer messages will give more details, such as possible leave dates and their living conditions in billets and military camps. But in general, postcards were a means of keeping in touch with home.

How: The 'how' of primary source analysis is 'How is the information contained within this primary source viewed by modern-day audiences. How does its information sit within the general view of this particular historical topic/theme?' So how does the postcard's message fit with what is known about, for example, trench warfare? Living conditions for the soldiers? The various battles of the First World War? Does the message add to this knowledge?

The aim of primary source analysis and the 6Ws is to squeeze as much as possible out of a source. Postcards sent home from the First World War are not just about what was written on the back or the picture shown on the front. Very often, the real information contained on a postcard is what was not written nor expressed.

Appendix III
Sample Postcard Analysis

The images on this page are the front and back of a postcard sent from the Western Front to an address in Chelmsford, Essex. The following page has an itemised analysis about each part of a postcard. Use this as a crib sheet to investigate a postcard sent during the First World War. A First World War postcard posted from a theatre of war consists of three categories of information: A) the details pre-printed on the postcard by the publisher/printer. B) the information written by the postcard's sender. C) Official information written or stamped on by an army officer or army post office.

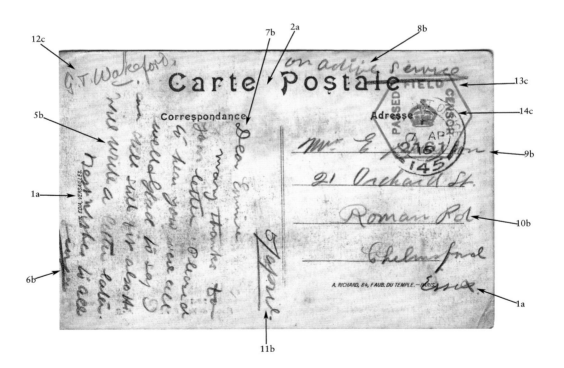

457. La Grande Guerre 1914-15-16
Environs de .... Pas-de-Calais, — La Ferme de TOUTVENT   A. R

Publisher/Printer Details

1. **Printer and/or publisher details.**
2. **Pre-printed heading (if any).** For example, Post Card, Carte Postale, Cartolina postale. What language; English, French, Italian? Another language? The language of any pre-printed text could help identify the country the sender was located in.
3. **The picture on the front side of the postcard.** Can this help identify the location of the postcard's sender? Although, if the picture is topographical view of a town or village, then this should be treated with caution as a soldier may have carried a packet of unwritten postcards as he marched from one area to another. A postcard with a view of a specific village/town does not necessarily mean that it was sent when a soldier was in or near that particular town (or even that he was in the same country as his postcard).
4. **Printed caption.** Does this help identify the location and/or the year? For example, because of the dates on its caption, this postcard cannot have been used before 1916.

Sender's Handwritten Details

5. **Message.** Is this in ink? In pencil? How does the handwriting look: carefully written or scrawled in a hurry? Could the writing implement (pen or pencil) indicate under what conditions the postcard was written: comfortable billet or in a supply trench? Is the message clearly written or with spelling mistakes and grammatical errors? Literate or illiterate writer? But does a badly written postcard necessarily mean an illiterate writer; or does it mean a writer under extreme stress and pre or post battle conditions?
6. **The sender's name.** This one is illegible; a legible name could help with research. If just a Christian name, can it be cross-referenced to the name of the recipient?

7. **The greeting** at the start of the message. Does this give an indication as to the relationship between the sender and the author? For example, 'Dear Mother and Father'.

8. **'On Active Service'** written by the sender. Sometimes abbreviated to 'O.A.S.', other times it was stamped on in ink. Writing this on a postcard or envelope ensured that postage did not have to be paid, but was sent free-of-charge.

9. **Name of the recipient.** If the sender hasn't written their surname at the end of their message, can the name of the recipient help with identifying the sender? Does the message give context to the recipient? For example, is this recipient the sender's mother, father, sister, brother? Has the sender written kisses (xxx) on the postcard? If he has, then this immediately implies a close relationship.

10. **Recipient's address.** Can the Census Returns for this address help identify the postcard's sender? Do not just check the 1911 Census, but also check returns for previous decades.

11. **Sender's own handwritten date.** Not always present, but if it is, even an incomplete handwritten date, coupled with the postmark and/or censor mark, could conclusively date a postcard.

Official Army and Post Office Details

12. **Censor's signature.** Is the censor's name in The National Archives' online *First World War Medal Index Cards*? If so, can information about the censor help?

13. **Ink-stamped censor mark.** In this case, a hexagon CM4 type. If the date of the postmark is unclear, then the censor mark type could identify the year.

14. **Dated postmark with its code.** In this case, it is unclear if this was a field or army post office postmark. Can this code be researched and identified?

15. **What, if anything, has been censored?** Can anything be read under the censor's blue pencil? Does enhancing it as digital image help? Digitally enhancing this postcard revealed the village name of Hébuterne under the censor's pencil. The fact that the name of the village had been censored gives a good indication that the sender of this postcard was somewhere nearby on 5 April 1916.

Bibliography

Primary Sources – The National Archives

Air combat reports: 49 Squadron, Royal Air Force (June 1918), AIR 1/1223/204/5/2634/89.
Air Ministry: Department of the Master-General of Personnel: Officers' Service Records – Charles Edward Pullen, AIR 76/414/76.
British Army Medal Index Cards, http://www.nationalarchives.gov.uk/help-with-your-research/research-guides/british-army-medal-index-cards-1914-1920/.
British Army Soldiers and officers in the First World War, WO 363.
Headquarters Branches and Services: Matron in Chief, WO95/3988-91[transcribed by Sue Light, http://www.scarletfinders.co.uk].
Lines of Communication Troops: War Diary of 14 General Hospital, WO95/4082/6.
Lines of Communication Troops: War Diary of 25 General Hospital, WO95/4085.
War Dairy 1/5th Battalion, South Lancashire Regiment: January 1916 – July 1919, WO 95/2929/2.
War Dairy: 1/7th Battalion, King's Liverpool Regiment: January 1916 – April 1919, WO 95/2927/1.
War Diary 9th Battalion East Lancashire Regiment, November 1915 to February 1919, WO 95/4851.

Primary Sources – Other

British Red Cross, *First World War Volunteers*, http://www.redcross.org.uk/About-us/Who-we-are/History-and-origin/First-World-War.
Commonwealth War Graves Commission, *War Dead*, http://www.cwgc.org/.

Printed Sources

The British Newspaper Archives, http://www.britishnewspaperarchive.co.uk/.

Secondary Sources – Books

Boyden, P. B., *Tommy Atkins' Letters: British Army Post: History of the British Army Postal Service from 1795*, (National Army Museum, 1990).
Collins, I., *An Illustrated History of the Embroidered Silk Postcard,* (Gabrian Antiques, 2001).

Daniel, F. W., *The Field Censor Systems of the Armies of the British Empire 1914–1918, Unit Allocations*, (Burnham on Crouch: Forces Postal History Society, 1984).

Doyle, P., *British Postcards of the First World War*, (Oxford: Shire Library, 2010).

Edmonds, J. E. (ed.), *Military Operations France and Belgium 1917: Messines and Third Ypres (Passchendaele)*, (Imperial War Museum: 1992).

James, N. D. G., *Gunners at Larkhill a History of the Royal School of Artillery*, (Gresham Books, 1983).

Kennedy, A. and Crabb, G., *Postal History of the British Army in World War I – before and after, 1903 to 1929*, (Epsom: George Crabb, 1977).

MacMillian, M., *Peacemakers: Six Months that Changed The World*, (London: John Murray, 2001).

Morris, J. *The German Air Raids on Great Britain 1914–1918*, (1925).

Pratt, E., *British Railways and the Great War*, (London: Selwyn and Blount Limited, 1921).

Proud, Edward B., *The History of the British Army Postal Service 1903–27*, (Dereham: Proud-Bailey Company Limited, 1983).

Wells, E. *Mailshot: A History of the Forces Postal Service*, (Defense Postal & Courier Services, 1987).

Wyrall, E. *The History of the King's Regiment (Liverpool Regiment), 1914–1919* (Edward Arnold & Co, 1928).

Secondary Sources – Websites*

49 Squadron Association, *49 Squadron*, (2016), http://www.49squadron.co.uk/home.

Allen, T., *Bruce Bairnsfather WW1 Postcards*, (2014), http://www.worldwar1postcards.com/bruce-bainsfather.php.

Allen, T., *Tommy's Mail & the Army Post Office*, http://www.worldwar1postcards.com/soldiers-mail.php.

Baker, C., *The Long, Long Trail*, (1996-2016) http://www.longlongtrail.co.uk/.

Billings, M., *The Influenza Pandemic of 1918*, (1997, revised 2005), https://virus.stanford.edu/uda/.

British Postal Museum & Archive, *The Post Office and the First World War*, http://www.postalheritage.org.uk/explore/history/firstworldwar/.

British Red Cross, *War-time volunteers and personnel records*, http://www.redcross.org.uk/About-us/Who-we-are/Museum-and-archives/resources-for-researchers/Volunteers-and-personnel-records.

Collins, I., *Embroidered Silk Postcards*, https://sites.google.com/site/embroideredsilkpostcards/home.

Commonwealth Graves Commission, *Find War Dead*, (2016), http://www.cwgc.org/

Forces Postal History Society, http://www.forcespostalhistorysociety.org.uk/index.html

Light Sue, *Scarlet Finders*, http://www.scarletfinders.co.uk/.

Lusitania Resource, *History, Passengers & Crew Biographies, and Lusitania Facts*, (2003-2016), http://www.rmslusitania.info/.

*All consulted 2016

Museum of the Order of St John, *Étaples Reports Project Introduction*, (2015), https://stjohnsgate.wordpress.com/category/etaples-reports-project-introduction/.

Preston Grammar School Association, *The Great War 1914-1918: War Memorial and Records*, (2008), http://www.ww1.pgsassociation.org.uk/.

Reznick, J. S., *The 'Convalescent Blues' in Frederick Cayley Robinson's 'Acts of Mercy'*, (2010), http://blog.wellcomelibrary.org/2010/06/the-convalescent-blues-in-frederick-cayley-robinsons-acts-of-mercy/.

Royal Air Force, *39 Squadron*, (2016), http://www.raf.mod.uk/organisation/39squadron.cfm.

University of Oxford, *The First World War Poetry Digital Archive: Map of Étaples Training Camp*, http://ww1lit.nsms.ox.ac.uk/ww1lit/gwa/document/9127/4558.

Royal Mail Group, *Charting the First World War – 1914* (2016), http://www.royalmailgroup.com/about-us/heritage/charting-first-world-war-1914.

Scally, H., *History Extra: 10 ways Christmas was celebrated during the First World War*, (2014), http://www.historyextra.com/feature/first-world-war/10-ways-christmas-was-celebrated-during-first-world-war.

Ships List, *Leyland Line Fleet*, (1997-2016) http://www.theshipslist.com/ships/lines/leyland.shtml.

Taft, Chris, *The Post Office in the First World War*, https://postalheritage.wordpress.com/2011/12/20/the-post-office-in-the-first-world-war.

Westminster Abbey, *Unknown Warrior*, (2016), http://www.westminster-abbey.org/our-history/people/unknown-warrior.

Index

Also available from Kate Cole and Amberley Publishing

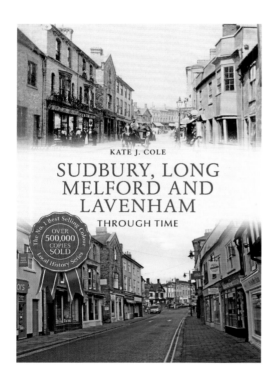

Sudbury, Long Melford and Lavenham Through Time

ISBN 9781445636801
eISBN 9781455636962

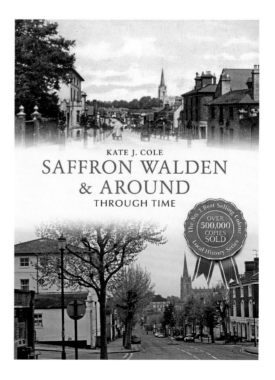

Saffron Walden & Around Through Time

ISBN 9781445636801
eISBN 9781455636962